TO OCRACOKE

*The author and his friend Lee
on holiday in Ocracoke*

TO OCRACOKE

BOYHOOD SUMMERS
ON THE OUTER BANKS

Fred Mallison

A CAROLINA CHILDHOOD : BOOK 2

SWEET BAY TREE BOOKS
COLUMBIA, NC
2000

TO OCRACOKE!
Boyhood Summers on the Outer Banks

A Carolina Childhood : Book 2

Published by

SWEET BAY TREE BOOKS
COLUMBIA, NC

Library of Congress Catalog Number 00-133437

ISBN 0-9643396-3-3

Printed and bound
in the USA

CONTENTS

This book is for
SISTER MARY and
AUNT LIZZIE

WITH GRATEFUL THANKS
to Rachel Mills
for helping edit the manuscript
and to Rachel & Jerry Mills
and Bland Simpson
for encouraging
the author.

ANTICIPATION

MY TRAVELS TO OCRACOKE BEGAN at a family conference around the supper table when I was about six. Mama asked Daddy to wait before he went to work in the vegetable garden. She wanted to talk about Ocracoke. "Can you come this year?"

"No," Daddy answered, "Not with Fred sick. But *you* go."

"*I* want to go," I injected. "I can swim and row a boat. I want to go this year."

"I don't think so, Mac. A house party for six or eight girls is all I can handle by myself. You can when you're older."

She turned to my brother Sammy and asked if he wanted to come along and help look after me. Sammy was appalled.

"Me? Be a nursemaid to him? Mama, you know I don't! I got a lot of things to do here."

I did not like that nurse idea any better than he did. Sister started to say something, but I interrupted her. "I ain't a baby"—"Am not," Mama injected automatically—"I'm six, goin' on seven!"

Mama and Sister began planning the July house party. Sister named the girls who wanted to go. They are all *old*, I thought, but most of them are pretty.

While Sister searched for her notebook, Aunt Lizzie joined the group at the table. She accepted a cup of coffee.

Daddy went out the back door and I started to follow him because I did not want to hear anymore about a trip I could not take. Mama gave me a message for Mary Young in the kitchen: "Tell Mary to clear the table and go on home. We'll be here for some time."

I delivered the message and complained, "They ain't goin' to take me."

Mary Young smiled at me. "Doan' be so sure. You wait and see." She pointed her finger at me and smiled again. I consoled myself by stuffing some cold biscuits in my pocket.

I helped Daddy mark some rows, then trudged over to the Otaheite tree beside the garage. I climbed up to sit and munch and sulk. I could see a lot but hear little from my spy post.

Through the window I saw Mama enter the kitchen and speak to Mary Young. I guessed she was telling Mary Young to go home, for Mary Young put on her coat and picked up her bundle. They came out to the end of the back porch where I could hear them.

"Where's that boy?" Mama asked.

"He gone out, Miss Nita. He mighty disappointed. Looked near 'bout sick." Mary Young was exaggerating in my favor. I kept quiet.

"If you see him, Mary, send him back in. I'll finish up here. We're still talking."

"Yes'm. I see Mr. Sam." Mary Young started to the garden. She met Daddy in the backyard. "Miss Nita wants to see that boy. Is he with you?"

"I'll find him," Daddy answered. As Mary Young started out the lane, he turned and looked straight up at me. "Come down," he called, and beckoned. I climbed down and followed him, still grumbling, "They ain't goin' to take me."

"Don't be so sure of that, Mac, and don't whine. We'll see

what happens. Come on in." He ruffled my hair. Daddy seemed to know something, as did Mary Young.

Mama, Sister, and Lizzie still sat around the dining room table. "Tell them we can still hold to a dollar a day," Mama told Sister. Mama lit a cigarette and sipped coffee while Sister scribbled away in her notebook. Aunt Lizzie wore her tight smile, the one she dispensed wholesale when people did what she thought they should.

"Sit down, Mac," Mama said, "and stop wiggling. You're going. Lizzie is going to take you and Mary in June. You can learn your way around the island and I'll come with the rest of the girls in July. Mind Lizzie!"

"Hot dog!" I hollered as I jumped up. I gave Lizzie and Mama a fast hug and gave Sister an affectionate hair pull. I rushed past Daddy, who had started upstairs, leaving him with a wave and a grin, and cut out for Bup's house.

All the grandchildren called Grandpa McIlhenny "Bup." He and I had talked a whole lot about Ocracoke, the boats, and his cottage.

"I'm goin', I'm goin'," I yelled as I ran into his yard. "Lizzie's takin' me and Sister in June before Mama comes."

Bup was crossing his back yard, his elbows pumping, matching his leg's strides. He congratulated me. "I told your Mother you were old enough. Good for Miss Lizzie. You'll like the whole island—especially the sail across the Sound." Grandpa began to grin. His body commenced to shake the way it did when he laughed inside.

"What is it, Bup? Tell me!" I said.

"You'll have a better crossing than old Woody Perkins had. He was the brickmason I took there to repair the chimney when I bought the place. We went in the *Lena Bell,* my old launch. It was a slow, rough trip and poor old Woody was seasick all the way down the river and across the Sound. When we landed, way after dark, he staggered ashore and fell right down in the sand.

He said the damndest thing I ever heard a grown man say: 'Long as I come this fur, Mr. Mac, I shore do hope I can see the Queen.'"

I laughed and worried at the same time. "I sure hope *I* don't get seasick."

"You won't," Bup assured me. "You'll be on a much bigger boat. It's a fine trip on the schooner."

Aunt Mary Bell called Grandpa to the telephone. He returned in a minute to tell me the call was from Mama. "She wants to know if 'that boy' is here talking about Ocracoke. She said to come home."

I am not sure in what year I made my first visit. I think it was 1931, but it could have been 1930. Sister Mary thought I visited the island even earlier with her and Mama, a visit of only a few days, but I have no recollection of it. It is possible that events of different visits blended in my memory.

Once having begun, I went to Ocracoke as long as the family vacationed there. What happened there follows, a series of semi-connected tales of good times during the hard times. A better place for good times has never been discovered.

BUGEYES

Wʜᴇɴ ᴛʜᴇ ʟᴀsᴛ ᴅᴀʏ ᴏғ sᴄʜᴏᴏʟ ғɪɴᴀʟʟʏ ᴄᴀᴍᴇ, my teacher was as happy as I was—and she was not even going to Ocracoke! The month of May had seemed longer than winter and each day passed slower than the week before Christmas.

I organized my own familiarization course on Ocracoke, asking so many questions that people began to avoid me. Both my father and grandfather talked grave-voiced to me about water safety and shipboard behavior. I even remembered what they said because they told me the same things, each in his own words. Condensed to fit in my head they were *Never act like a fool on the water.*

Aunt Lizzie told me about the island, about Verrazzano and Sir Walter Raleigh and old Blackbeard. She read to me about the Indians from a book written long ago by a man named Lawson who called the island *Occacock.* The Indians, Aunt Lizzie said, called it *Woccocon.* I had heard so many Ocracoke stories at family gatherings that I began to think I knew all about the place.

On Saturdays I hung around the docks and identified the Ocracoke boats. On one bright, shining day I even got on a boat by helping a man I knew carry some boxes aboard. Mr. Garrish, the mate, met us, and we all three climbed down a ladder into what my friend and the mate called the hold. I was entranced to be poking around the inside of the boat, and stayed until the men called me out. I liked the smell down there, a new smell. It was sort of an ocean and grocery-store aroma. I learned all about the boats in preparation for the great voyage.

There were two Washington-to-Ocracoke boats: sixty-five feet long, two-masted sailing vessels with small auxiliary engines. They were called "Chesapeake Bay bugeyes," a name I savored. Neither Daddy nor Grandpa knew just why they were called bugeyes, so I was satisfied that nobody in the world knew. The vessels had been modified from their original design as large oyster dredgers by having the forward scuttle and hatch removed and a cabin built in their place. The captain's and mate's quarters were in the rear cabin.

Captain Ike O'Neal skippered the *Russell L.* and Captain Dave Williams sailed the *Preston*. The boats looked identical to me, so I learned to look for the names on the carved trail boards above their eager clipper bows. The captains were easier to distinguish, for Captain Dave had a white mustache, while Captain Ike was red-headed and red-faced. Both captains and mates lived at Ocracoke, and I was surprised to learn that on the island the Ocracoke boat was known as the Washington boat. I adopted that terminology as my own, wanting to sound like an experienced visitor or even an islander.

The two captains coordinated their schedules so each vessel made one trip each week. The bugeyes came up from Ocracoke the day before their departure from Washington and lay at the dock overnight, allowing time for cargo handling. Each vessel left Washington laden with cases of canned goods, fresh groceries, hardware, dry goods, sometimes lumber or barrels of fuel, and anything else the islanders needed. The Ocracokers shipped their products to Washington: kegs of corned mullet, barrels of fresh fish, and, in season, tubs of oysters. Washingtonians preferred

Ocracoke oysters over all others. One oyster customer asked Mr. Garrish why Ocracoke oysters were bigger and more select than others. "Because they're refreshed twice a day," he answered. He explained that the tides swept over the oyster beds with clean ocean water so they grew bigger and fatter.

There were usually more passengers on Saturdays—and hence more revenue—so the captains alternated the schedules of the Saturday and Wednesday departures. My family always sailed down on the Saturday boat and most often returned on the mid-week daytime boat. The day and night crossings seemed entirely different voyages, yet we sailed across the same waters.

The Saturday night departure from Fowle's dock was at nine o'clock, and it was a bustling, social occasion. Family members left behind, friends, and envious onlookers came to bid the travelers farewell. Passengers rushed last-minute baggage aboard or searched frantically for misplaced bundles, children cavorted, and grown-ups tried to suppress their excitement. Daddy always came to see us off. Midsummer was tobacco curing and tobacco flue season, the busiest time of the year, because Daddy's farms grew tobacco and the store manufactured tobacco flues.

Mama or Aunt Lizzie would take charge of the group, managing to establish headquarters on the forward-hatch cover, long known to them as the choice spot. The after-hatch was second best because the front one was better protected from spray by the foremast and passenger cabin. Usually first-timers for the voyage claimed space in the cabin. They were often people from up the state and unused to boats. Daddy called them "highland terrapins" and Uncle Tom, his brother, referred to them as "haymaker's mates." In any case, the cabin was a place to avoid, a refuge used only during the heaviest rain squall. Inside, the air was hot and close and one of the terrapins could always be relied upon to vomit on the floor, thus starting an epidemic.

I always stayed on deck. In case of rain the captain or mate spread a tarpaulin over the hatch-dwellers. The hatch was both lounge and dining table, for Mama or Lizzie would bring a big picnic basket for a midnight snack. It was more than a snack and more fun than a picnic, more of a banquet than a supper. The ladies pulled out boxes and plates of fried chicken, ham biscuits, potato salad, and deviled eggs. They produced cheese sandwiches, pickles, pie, and cake. There were cool drinks, iced tea, and hot coffee. I liked to drink some of the ship's water, uniquely flavored, that I dipped out of a white-painted barrel with a canvas flap over its little hatch.

The boat left the dock under engine power, as the captain conned her through the draw in the railroad bridge and down river to wider waters. If the wind served, as it usually did, captain and mate hoisted sails and shut down the engine when the ship came abreast of Chocowinity Bay or Blount's Creek. Then the real fun began, for the old bugeyes were brisk sailers.

The swooping glide of the hull up and down again, the cant of the deck that rolled cups and glasses off the hatch cover, the swish of the bow wave, were all delights. I learned to slip away from the hatch cover, scramble forward past the cabin and sit a-straddle the inboard section of the bowsprit where the swoop and swish were maximum. At first my sojourn on the bowsprit was short, for one of Mama's agents would retrieve me, or I would be displaced by dictatorial teenagers. I eventually earned the trust of my elders and the boats' captains by my careful shipboard behavior. It was worthwhile minding to gain the freedom of the bow. Also, there was the weight of father-grandfather instructions. The young couples who displaced me were a different problem, but I learned to outwait and outwit them. I sat by the mast just behind them and sang, or rather croaked, or whistled to myself. The intruders usually left in disgust to seek a more private nook. Fortunately, nobody threw me overboard.

I liked to lie on deck with my head over the low rail, looking down at the bow cutting the waves. It was best in the Sound where the rollers were big and regular. The stem would start to bury itself in the front of a wave, the dark waters rise to meet me, the spray fly sideways. Then the bow rose over the wave, carrying me up, up, with the water receding below. The water was black, but the foam and spray were white. I would watch the thick curl of white slant back from each side of the cutwater, and think of it as the ship's mustache, like Captain Dave's. The sea stories I read later called it "a bone in her teeth," but I continued to think of the ship's mustache.

In the moonlight, the foam was still white, but the Sound was dark green. The waves ahead appeared almost semi solid until the stem cut them in green slices, edged with white meringue. The little wavelets on top of the big swells, reflecting the moonlight, were the bronze-green of Scuppernong grapes. (That was as close as I got to imagining a "wine-dark sea.") Lying there on deck, the gray jib swelling above me, the green rollers below, I imagined myself transported to foreign seas. I was in the bows of *Santa Maria*, gazing ahead for sight of the shores of Cathay, or with Leif Ericsson pressing on to Vinland. I sailed my galley across the Mediterranean searching for Turks, or shipped in a frigate bound for Tahiti. I circled the globe on the Ocracoke boat.

Sleep would finally overcome dreams of the sea, and I rolled up in a blanket on the hatch cover that had become a bed. Sometimes my naps were broken by changes in the wind, the boat's motion, or rain. It was fun to snuggle down under the tarpaulin with just my nose stuck out.

On one dreadful occasion Mama sent me below to avoid a heavy rain storm. I crawled in a vacant bunk in the stuffy cabin and tried to go to sleep. My doze was terminated by a funny feeling in my middle, a cold sweat, and a swelling sensation in my head and neck. Violent, unmanageable nausea came, as my color changed and my freckles stood out in bas-relief. I came out of that cabin like a rocket, pointed my muzzle over the side and let it all go. I thought I might have splattered somebody on shore. The rain felt good, the wind felt good, and I quickly recovered, but I did not go back down in that cabin again.

Cousin Nena once had a similar experience. Seized by sea-sickness in the cabin, she rushed on deck followed by her sister Betsy. She lay over the low rail with half her body over the side and with her big sister sitting on her legs to hold her in place. Captain Ike spotted them from his position aft at the wheel. The horrified captain tore foreward to pull them back on deck.

On that first trip with Lizzie there was no rain, no storm, and no seasickness. Sister and her friend Margaret escorted me to the bowsprit for a brief visit, but thereafter I ventured there alone.

I was wide awake before sunrise. I did not want to miss anything. Lizzie was still sleeping, ruler straight with her ankles neatly crossed and a blanket over her middle; Sister and Margaret were talking in low tones. It sounded like they were saying things like swishing and swashing.

"What are you-all talkin' about, Sister?" I had to chime in. "What's a swash and what's swishing?"

"The swash is a sort of a reef that we have to cross. We like to say we're *swishing the swash* when we cross it."

I knew what a reef was. Lizzie had read me a poem about a terrible shipwreck on a reef, and I was excited to learn there was one at Ocracoke.

"Is it like 'the reef of Norman's woe,' Sister?" All I could think about was rocks and breakers. I imagined seeing a ship—some other ship, not ours of course—wrecked on the rocks.

Lizzie, now awake, answered my question. "Certainly not!" she said, "It's just a sandbar, Mac. There's no problem. Captain O'Neal knows just what to do. Mary Bishop, you might have said it's just a shallow place!"

Sunrise came and the captain did indeed show us just what to do. When the ship drew close to the island, he turned and sailed along the shore, but a long way out. I could see houses and trees and wondered why we did not go straight ashore, though I did not want to ask. Captain Ike and the mate started the engine and lowered the sails. In a few more minutes they did steer for the island, but the boat was past all the houses. She turned again, close inshore, and headed for a long pier near the first of the houses.

"Where's the reef, Lizzie?" I asked.

"Look over to the left," she answered. "That long yellow streak. That's the reef. It looks yellow where the water is shallow. It's yellow sand. The rocks of Norman's woe, indeed!"

The long pier was the dock of the Pamlico Inn, Cap'n Bill Gaskill's hostel. The *Russell L.* had passengers and freight to unload here. I jumped up on the dock, anxious to land on Ocracoke. Aunt Lizzie called me back. We were not going to land here. Aunt Ella's cottage, where we would stay, was at the far end of the Sound shore. I fidgeted while most of the passengers and baggage debarked. Mr. Garrish cast off the lines and *Russell L.* chugged further down the shore, past houses nestled in the trees and houses built near the beach.

By the time the big bugeye slowly nosed in the narrow Creek entrance by the Coast Guard Station, I was jumping with excitement. The boat docked at a pier jutting out from the left-hand shore. This time we did land. My exploration of Ocracoke began that day, lasted for years, and never was entirely completed.

ARRIVAL ON THE ISLAND

ONCE ASHORE, LIZZIE CONFERRED with the owner of one of the island's secondary public transit units. After boats and skiffs, the most useful craft were small, stripped-down, flatbed trucks. They had big tires kept soft to better negotiate the sandy trails, and could go anywhere a boat could not. Sister, Margaret, and I helped load our things and climbed on the back, while Aunt Lizzie sat in the cab with the driver. Away we went, through tree-shaded tunnels, across sandy flats, around the harbor and over to the Sound shore from the rear. Sister held on to my belt as I stood, craned, and twisted to see everything.

We piled the baggage on the front porch, Lizzie paid Mr. Gaskill for hauling us, and we all stood on the porch and looked around.

"The breeze is as wonderful as ever," Aunt Lizzie announced.

"It is," Sister agreed, "and it's wonderful to be back. Everything looks the same."

Margaret, peering along the beach, said," I wonder who those three boys are 'way over there. Are they the ones from Belhaven?" Sister looked, too. I was busy looking at geography.

I gulped in the breeze. It was the same wind as at home, but it sure was stronger. It blew in my face as I looked across the Sound at another island 'way off. I conceded that it smelled fresher than the town breeze.

"Let's get unpacked," Lizzie urged. "Do you girls want to take an upstairs room? Mac, put your things in the back room. I'll take this front one," she pointed the way. I carried my two boxes in my room, then explored the rest of the house. All the rooms, once the windows were opened, were full of wind.

We were staying in Aunt Ella's cottage, because Grandpa's was rented to someone else for June. Aunt Lizzie pointed out where it was and Sister told me we would walk over there after lunch. "I'll take you to Cap'n Bill's and Gary Bragg's, too."

Lizzie added, "We'll go 'round the Creek to the Post Office tomorrow." The geography lesson had begun; it was better than in a book.

I was not really lonesome with Lizzie and Sister and Margaret, but I thought it would be nice to have a buddy of my own to help explore. I saw several island boys my age, passing the cottage, or helping adults with boats or nets or stuff like that. I said hello or waved and they responded, but they seemed busy with their own affairs. The island boys had learned not to expect instant friendship from visitors, for their friendliness might not be genuine and they might be gone tomorrow. Each side looked at the other sideways as they spoke briefly. Islander-visitor friendships were slow to mature, but they would come.

I found plenty to do by myself. Lizzie had brought hand-lines, so I could fish from the piers. I learned to crab in the shallow water and to beachcomb for all sorts of interesting things washed up on shore. I spent a lot of time swimming in the Sound, with the others and alone as long as I kept close to the cottage. If barnacles grew on people I would have had them! I sometimes forgot Aunt Lizzie's eagle-eye and swam too far out, too close to the channel. When Lizzie hailed, I heard and came in. Later on, I became more adept at avoiding observation, but Aunt Lizzie was hard to fool.

Aunt Ella had a small, flat-bottomed skiff, and I was confident I knew all there was to know about rowing a boat. Even so, Lizzie would not let me take the boat out alone, so I had to depend on her or Sister to go with me.

One day Sister, Margaret, and I rowed farther out in the Sound than usual. Sister and Margaret, seated side by side, were each pulling an oar. Sister's oar broke water; she slipped and fell off the seat. Margaret shrieked with mirth and lost her oar overboard. Then, being seventeen, they could not stop laughing. They sat in the bottom of the boat, helpless with hilarity. I did not quite comprehend what was so funny, but joined in anyhow. What fun we were having while the ebbing tide urged the skiff toward the inlet.

Fortunately we were being watched. One of the island men, Lum Gaskill, waded out to his skiff, poled rapidly through the shallows, then rowed out to the goofy sailors. He took us in tow, picked up the lost oar, and pulled us back to shore. After making both skiffs fast to their mooring posts, he waded ashore, put hands on hips, and gave the subdued sailors a glare and a slow, disgusted shake of his head. He turned and strode off down the shore, not having spoken a word the whole time. Aunt Lizzie, who always found out everything, spoke several later.

I discovered two irresistible attractions my first day on the island. The first was a big sail boat, high and apparently dry, in a grassy field behind the cottage. It looked just like the boat that brought us to the island. The other thing was a great big vacant house on the point just by the Creek entrance. At the supper table, I asked about these tantalizing landmarks.

"I don't know whose schooner it is. It wasn't there the last time I came. It belongs to somebody, though, so you'd best stay away from it—besides, it's in a marsh. I'll ask about it."

Lizzie put down her knife and fork. "I can tell you about the house. It's the Doxsee house. It was a private home, then a hotel, then a cannery. It's falling down and full of rusty nails. Better not prowl around there either."

The girls began to talk about something else. I silently observed that the old boat could not sink and all houses were full of nails. I did, however, have to admit to myself that rusty nails had an affinity for my feet. I nodded to Lizzie signifying the reception of her advice.

The day came soon enough when Lizzie went 'round the Creek and Sister and Margaret went visiting up the beach. Lizzie instructed me on leaving, "Stay close to the cottage, Mac, and don't go swimming until I get back."

"Okay," I said. Rationalizing that "close" meant "in sight of" and "no swimming" meant "not way out," I prepared to explore.

First, I decided, the boat in the field. The grassy field, close up, was not what it looked like. The grass turned out to be spike rushes and taller spartina grass. I learned at once not to let the spike rushes get up my pants leg. The rushes grew in clumps like little islands with clear water in between. The little islands were so stubbly-prickly, so I returned to the house for my shoes. When I wore shoes on the island, they were always the rubber and canvas kind that became fragrant if not often washed. I called them tennis shoes although I had never seen a game of tennis. (For like reason, I called the knitted short-sleeved shirts I wore polo shirts, but did not play polo either.)

Shoes on, I started toward the boat, its round red bottom shining in the sun. The boat was canted away from me, so I would have to go around the end to climb up on deck. I made slow progress, jumping from hummock to hummock, clutching handfuls of rushes to keep my balance. Before long my foot slipped and I plunged thigh-deep in watery mud. I scrambled back onto the hummock and resumed my frog-hop. The rush clumps were further apart as I progressed and the jumps longer.

I kept slipping. On my fourth or fifth slip, I fell backwards in neck-deep mud pudding. I was not afraid of deep water and liked swimming, but this mess was something else. Climbing back on the reed hummock, I craned my neck to survey ahead and behind. I was barely halfway. I was also slimy, black, and sordid from neck to heels. I turned back, planning as I hopped, to bring somebody else and two boards another time.

My immediate problem on regaining the sandy shore was to clean up before Aunt Lizzie returned. The simple solution to the problem was to go swimming in my clothes. So I threshed and swiddled clean, then waded ashore to decide what to do next after my clothes dried out. I might as well explore the Doxsee house and round out the afternoon with the other forbidden fruit.

Shoes were still necessary, as the shore and yard were paved with clam and oyster shells. The big old house was nearly a ruin, as Lizzie had said. The front porch, both roof and floor, had fallen down and most of the boards had been carried away. I stepped carefully, as there were still a lot of broken planks with rusty nails poking through them. I remembered Lizzie's advice and I also remembered lying face-down on Dr. Rodman's cold leather couch back at home last winter being jabbed in the bottom with a needle because of a rusty nail. Care was better than needles.

There were no steps nor front door, so I climbed up onto the door sill and ventured inside. I was in a central hall facing the stairs to the second floor, with rooms on each side and the long, dark hall ahead. The floors were littered with broken glass, scraps of wood and old papers. Little sand dunes grew on the floor in front of some of the shattered windows. First I explored the hall leading to the rear rooms. There was another staircase back there. The rooms with boarded-over windows were black. Something creaked. I froze, listened, my heart pounding, until I realized it was only a loose shutter. Even so, I thought I would cut short this visit. Lizzie or Sister might come back soon.

I trotted up the back stair, through the upstairs hall past more empty rooms, then down the front stair and out to the shell yard. I had found no ghosts, no skeletons, no bloodstains, but I knew it was a good haunted house and I would come back to it.

When Aunt Lizzie returned, she found me sitting on the porch swinging my legs and watching the gulls, the very picture of an obedient child.

Lizzie was sharp-eyed. "You look damp, Mac." She felt my shirt. "And how in the world did you get mud under your collar?"

"I fell down in the mud back there," I answered. "Back there where those mud fiddlers are."

"Humph," said Lizzie. "Maybe. Come change your clothes." I always tried to tell Aunt Lizzie the truth as far as I went, but not necessarily the whole truth unless I was cornered into it. I really had fallen in the mud, I reasoned, and there were mud fiddlers *somewhere* back there.

Sister and Margaret sometimes went out after supper to the square dance or to visit friends. I usually stayed home with Lizzie. Aunt Lizzie liked to read aloud as much as I liked to listen. After supper she would light the extra bright Aladdin oil lamp, place it on the table, move her rocking chair alongside, and adjust her footstool. She read for an hour or two until my eyelids sagged. Aunt Lizzie had firm opinions on literature as well as everything else. She would not read what she called trashy children's books. She read me Uncle Remus stories with correct unexaggerated accents and varied the evenings with Sir Walter Scott's tales of adventure. It might have been unusual, but Uncle Remus and Sir Walter got along well with each other.

June seemed such a short month. I was reluctant to leave Lizzie and the good times in Ella's cottage, even though I knew I would move up the shore for another month with Mama. The leave-taking was made easier by the anticipation of the big house party at Bup's cottage and the new people I would meet there. It was the beginning of my love of the island and my understanding of why all my kin folks talked about Ocracoke so much.

PLACES & PEOPLE

THE CREEK'S MOUTH WAS THE STARTING POINT for my own survey of the island. When, years later, people began to call the Creek "Silver Lake," I had to re-adjust my thinking. I resisted the change. The Sound shore ran in a gentle crescent southward from the mouth of the Creek to the Pamlico Inn, and in another curve to Springer's Point, about a mile or a little less. The landmark at the Creek end was the Doxsee house.

Lizzie had told me what it had been and somebody else said it was once a clam factory. I thought it was funny to call it a factory when it did not manufacture the clams but only canned them. Anyhow, that accounted for all those shells that covered the yard, the shore, and out in the water. The ban on the Doxsee house was not mentioned in succeeding summers, so my buddies and I could visit it at will.

A hundred yards from the Doxsee house was Aunt Annie's cottage, an A-roofed box with a big cement block of a front porch. Next to that was Aunt Ella's, the house that Lizzie used on most of her visits. Uncle Dave Lucas and Aunt Ella had bought the house from Seth Bridgeman, who had visited the West Indies in his youth and noted the architecture there. The cottage had a high peaked roof and wide front and back porches, their rafters left exposed. In the second floor rooms, low down, almost at the floor, were windows opening under the porch roofs. The breeze was funneled up under the front porch roof, through the windows into the upstairs rooms and out under the back porch roof. All rooms, upstairs and down, had through ventilation. It was the most comfortable summer house I have ever stayed in. Uncle Ed said, with the windows all shut it was cozy in the wintertime too.

Uncle Ed had lived there one winter all by himself, I knew, because of some family problems. He stayed there the next summer, too, so Lizzie had to rent Bup's cottage to give her brother the solitude he craved just then. Uncle Ed was the finest story teller I ever knew. He loved to spin his tales to an audience of children, holding them spellbound with adventure, humor, or mystery. His stories were suitable for children, never coarse, but often just racy enough to appeal to small boys.

The tale about Uncle Ed's friend who was injured in the war was a good one. It was a story for boys only. The man was near an exploding shell, Uncle Ed said, and had several of his parts blown off, namely his big toe, his forefinger, his nose, and his male member, which Uncle Ed politely called his turkeypease. The army doctors were overworked during the battle and maybe dumb, too. The poor shell-shocked soldier was brought in by the stretcher bearers and laid on the operating table, together with his blown off parts. The harassed doctors quickly stitched back the detached items and sent the man back home. The poor fellow, Uncle Ed related, was ever after troubled by his war wounds, for the doctors had sewn the things in the wrong places.

His big toe was placed in the spot where his nose had been, making it hard for him to cut his toenail without going cross-eyed. His nose was affixed to his hand in place of his forefinger and it was embarrassing to take out his handkerchief and blow his hand. The new place where his forefinger was growing made it even more embarrassing to open his pants to point directions. The poor old soldier could hardly unbutton his own trousers using his nose and thumb to do it. The audience always waited in suspence for Uncle Ed's final comment about how the poor fellow had to take off his shoe and sock whenever he had to pee. My buddies and I often asked Uncle Ed to repeat this sad, hilarious tale and he would vary the parts' new locations with other embarrassments. All this happened before the advent of medical malpractice suits, which could have added more chapters about the poor man explaining and demonstrating his misfortunes from the witness chair.

Uncle Ed told other stories which were suitable for boys and girls, like the one about bringing up the devil. Uncle Ed said he had once stopped at a house in the country to get a drink of water from the well. When he drew close to the well, a small swarm of children came out of hiding and warned him to be careful. "There's a haint in there," some said. Another little boy, the big whites of his eyes glaring, told him "T'ain't a haint. H'its de devil." Others agreed. Uncle Ed saw the bucket was down in the well. He heard a low rumbling growl. The little kids backed away, round-eyed and watchful. A rope led out of the well, through a pulley overhead and down to a hand-cranked windlass. He cranked the windlass one turn, calling "What's down there?" A sort of howl, screech and roar answered him, a sound nothing human could make. The kids backed farther away. As Uncle Ed cranked slowly, the din increased. He stood back as far as he could and still turn the crank. Up came the well bucket revealing a black alley cat, fur spiked out to twice the size a cat should be, screeching and spitting his rage. The cat flashed over the well curb faster than a bolt of lightning and disappeared. The little children crowded up to the well. "H'it was de debble, warn't it Mister?" one asked. Uncle Ed agreed that it was.

About a hundred yards across the marsh where the wrecked sail boat lay was higher ground and more houses. The marsh drained into the Creek, so the Sound beach was not marshy, but it was narrow. There were no cottages right on the Sound shore along this stretch. Small trees—myrtle, yaupon, and yucca—edged the beach, which was clean white sand with occasional outcroppings of black turf or peat. Back from the shore the trees were taller, the ground higher, and houses were scattered through the groves.

The Nunnelee cottage was the next one up the beach, a brown, shingle-covered house very close to the water. House parties from home often rented the Nunnelee cottage, so I visited there many times. During a later summer it was rented by some people named Anderson who were stopping while en route in their sail boat to the West Indies. Aunt Lizzie knew the Andersons and took us to meet them and hear all about their cruise. Right away I tried to promote a trip on their boat, but was disappointed to learn it was on the mainland being repaired. We would have to go home before the Andersons' boat was returned.

My friend Lee was with me that trip, and he cut his toe one day near the Andersons' cottage. Mrs. Anderson doctored the wound for him, patted his cheek, and said it was "an awful shame" (rhymimg awful with waffle). Lee was highly embarrased, I was gleeful, and the two of us later shamefully mocked the kind lady by dubbing any untoward event "an affle shame." We were learning various new dialects during the summers on the island: the Ocracokers' talk; that of Black people from different places; certain Yankees' alien accents; plus the pleasant sound of the Andersons, which may have been Yankee tempered with Scandinavian. If we could imitate the sound, we mocked them all.

Behind the Nunnelee cottage, back in the trees, was Bup's second rental cottage, rarely visited by me, for my family used Bup's first cottage, which was a little farther along the shore. The second cottage was set about a hundred yards back from the water, with some little trees and bushes in front of it.

Bup's first house had the same screened windows under the porch roof as Aunt Ella's house, but the roof was not as steeply pitched so it was not quite as well ventilated upstairs. It did have more porch: a wide front porch joined on each end to side porches and a separate back porch. At the back end of each side porch was a room with windows and a door from the porch. These were the overflow bedrooms. One of them had been reserved for Uncle Joe's summer bedroom, but he died after my first summer on the island so I sometimes used it. Bup's house was divided into a big living-dining room in front with a bedroom to one side and a large kitchen on the right rear. On the left rear was a smaller room, dark because of only one window, that was sometimes a breakfast room, sometimes a bedroom. Upstairs were two large bedrooms that were the exclusive territory of Sister and the girls.

Few of the Ocracoke houses had indoor plumbing in those days. Our back porch boasted a pitcher pump that furnished a flow of undrinkable dark water which could be used for washing. The water was not contaminated, it just tasted awful. Drinking water was collected rain water, drained from the roof into a cistern or rain barrels. When that ran low somebody had to go either to the nearest neighbors', the Braggs, and fill buckets at their pump, or a little farther off to Mr. Ballance's, who had the best-tasting water on that part of the island. I became adept at vanishing when the call sounded for a bucket of drinking water. I particularly disliked going to Mr. Ballance's. Although Mr. Ballance was a friendly man who made visitors and water-haulers welcome, he had a goat in his yard with whom I shared a mutual antipathy. In other words, I was scared of the goat and the goat knew it. (Brother Sammy had told me the goat was fierce.)

With no water system there was no washing machine nor even a laundry room. Each person had to hand-launder his own socks and underwear in a washtub on the back porch. Sheets, shirts, dresses, and things were carried to one of the island ladies who took in washing. I had no laundry problems, because I seldom wore underwear or socks. My dress was refined to the essentials. A pair of short khaki pants and a short sleeved shirt were all that was necessary. The shirt was prescribed to prevent blistering in the sun, and my mother equipped me with a round straw hat which I scorned and misplaced as soon as possible. The hat either blew off or got in the way.

There was no problem washing the pants and shirts. I got dirty daily or even hourly, but I found a simple solution. The wide Sound sparkled fifty yards from the front door and I loved swimming. My bathing suit was a one-piece woolen cover that encased the body from thighs to strapped shoulders. It itched intolerably when dry and it was a lot of trouble to go back to the house to put the thing on. There were piers out front and rock jetties reaching out from the shore. It was no trouble at all to fall overboard. I averaged falling off the piers or the rocks six times a day. My clothes stayed reasonably clean from the frequent swishings and quickly dried in the sun and breeze, though my trousers were probably not well creased.

The other non-existent plumbing was a bathroom—a toilet. Ocracoke cottages had the usual "necessary house" in their backyards. Aunt Ella's was on the very edge of the salt marsh and was equipped with mud fiddlers underneath. The boy's game of bombing mud fiddlers does not bear discussion.

Bup's cottage had no bathroom and no backhouse either. There had been one, but it was gone. The closest neighbors, Mr. and Mrs. Gary Bragg, lived very close indeed to the left rear of Bup's house. The Braggs ran a large boarding house. To increase their capacity, they had built a small detached cottage in the corner of their front yard. It was much sought after. However, the most prominent view from the new guest cottage was Bup's backhouse. The Braggs had recently installed a generator, a water system, and indoor plumbing. Only a few buildings on the island had such improvements, probably only the lighthouse keepers' house, the Coast Guard Station, and the Pamlico Inn.

Mr. Bragg made Bup a proposition. Bup's house guests would have the near exclusive use of Mr. Braggs old jumbo-sized, four-holer privy if Bup would tear down and fill in his old one. Bup agreed and everybody thought it was worth the extra walk to sit in such a nice place covered with morning glories and honey-suckle. Mr. Bragg had installed some sort of chemical treatment in his grand old privy. It still smelled, but it smelled different. (Later on, I would think of Mr. Bragg's chemical toilet whenever I smelled espresso coffee.)

The next place of importance on the Sound shore was the Pamlico Inn, generally referred to as Cap'n Bill's. I heard some-body refer to the Inn as Washington's headquarters on the island. I chewed on that thought for a while, and finally asked Lizzie if they meant George Washington. She answered that President Washington had never visited Ocracoke. Poor George Washing-ton, I thought.

The Inn, to me, looked huge and architecturally perfect. It was a large, plain, and functional three-winged building, enclosing three sides of a square. Across the back of the square were the kitchen, dining room, and the Gaskill family's quarters. At each back corner were bathrooms and shower rooms. Along each side of the courtyard was a stack of guest rooms, two rooms high and one room thick, tied together with wide first-floor and second-floor porches. The open side of the square faced the Sound. At its center, a dock extended out to the channel. I was delighted to hear somebody say it was called "Teach's Hole Channel." From what I had heard, I sort of admired old Blackbeard.

Part way out the dock was the dance pavilion, the social cen-ter of the island. It was joined to one side of the dock and stood long-legged on pilings. The pavilion was a many-shuttered frame building, smooth-floored and open-raftered, with benches around three sides. A small bandstand and a snack bar filled in the fourth side. A few people, grown-ups and children, were usually sitting around during the day. Whenever I scrounged a nickel I stopped by for a "co-cola" or one of the more colorful grape, orange, or cherry pops.

My friends and I never had or needed much money. An occasional cool drink or ice cream was all I ever bought. One time, though, I was loaded with money and treated everybody as long as my fortune lasted. This happened after a heavy storm had rolled a lot of lagan up on the shore. I customarily explored the tide line after storms. I picked up, out of a mop of seaweed, a large green bottle encrusted with fruit, leaf, and flower designs in the glass. A tourist-looking man accosted me as I stood admiring my find and offered me fifty cents for the treasure. I took it and took off for the cool drink counter.

This lucky sale made me consider the commercial possibilities of beachcombing. Storm tides deposited all sorts of things, but when I began to search seriously for saleable objects I found little. I managed to collect a stock of plain-looking whiskey and beer bottles, a few small milk bottles, and some pickle jars. I found almost a dozen cypress shingles and a belt with no buckle. Dead fish did not count. I arranged my inventory in a tasteful display on a corner of the porch and eagerly awaited customers. Nobody offered to buy anything. Some days later Mama made me throw my stock in the trash barrel. I complied grumpily except for the shingles, which I shoved under the porch for future use.

I attended many square dances at the pavilion as a spectator. Lots of people just sat on the benches and watched. Sister and the girls loved to dance, as did the island boys and girls and many visitors. People of all ages enjoyed the dancing, I noticed, including my visiting aunts and uncles. Mama often, Aunt Lizzie less frequently, attended the dances if their girls were there, but they did not dance. I sat there, tapping my foot to the music, trying to get up the nerve to ask Sister to let me try it with her. I learned most of the steps that were called, but I never practiced them. I just watched, keeping time with my toes, and breathed in the clean, salty, sea breeze blowing through the open shutters. The sound and smell of the pavilion linger in my memory. At the back of the Pamlico Inn's courtyard, near the dining room I liked to sniff the rich peppery aroma. The Pamlico Inn smelled good at both ends.

The shore between Mr. Bragg's pier and Cap'n Bill's was always a busy place, with fishnets drying on racks, boats tied out to posts, or drawn up on the shore. People worked there repairing nets, painting skiffs, or other interesting things. They did not mind being watched as long as the watchers did not interfere. A path ran along this stretch of shore and turned inland toward Bup's cottage.

Between the Inn and the cottage were two ditches to cross. The first one, nearest the Inn, was enclosed in wooden walls and was crossed by a stile. It drained a marsh behind the Inn and also carried the run-off from the shower rooms. After a rainstorm it was a torrent, but it was not an attractive ditch because those wooden walls made it hard to climb out of, especially when it was soapy. My gang of buddies called this one the wood ditch or the stile ditch.

Further along toward Bup's the path turned sharply and crooked its way through a grove of small trees and bushes, a part of the same marsh, and crossed another ditch. This one, wide, muddy, and tranquil, was much more charming than the wood ditch. We named it the Turtle Ditch, for from its banks we caught, admired, and threw back ugly black turtles the size of saucers. My buddy Billy knew a lot about science—biology, herpetology, whatever. Even if Billy was not sure about the answer to a question, he would dredge up an answer anyhow. These turtles, Billy assured me, were known as horseturd terrapins. Both of us were surprised at the girls' hilarity when Billy told them the name. We tried to explain that it was a scientific name, but those ignorant girls would not listen.

When anybody crossed the Turtle Ditch at night, he needed a flashlight, for the path was dark and crooked. If no flashlight was handy, a wise traveller learned to wait until the beam of the lighthouse swiveled 'round and illuminated the crossing. One cloudy night Mama returned from the square dance alone. The batteries in her light were weak, the overcast masked the lighthouse, and she stumbled in the Turtle Ditch. She climbed out wet, muddy, and mad. Fortunately for her pride, of which she had a large stock, nobody witnessed her fall. She hurried home and cleaned up before anybody else arrived. Mama had a good sense of humor, so she did not hesitate to tell the story on herself, but she wanted to be the one to tell it and not some guffawing bystander.

Along the Sound shore at irregular intervals were long jetties built of mostly rounded waterworn rocks, ranging from cantaloupe to watermelon size. A lot of small creatures lived in the crevices of the rock jetties. We liked to peer and pry at the little caves to discover fish, eels, crabs, little rounded stone crabs, mussels, and barnacles. Bup explained to me where the rocks came from. Ships, he said, brought them in when they were carrying a light cargo and dropped them on shore when they were loading a heavy cargo or wanted to be light enough to sail in the shallow parts of the Sound. Sailing ships, Bup said, needed heavy weights in their bottoms to keep from turning over in a strong wind. Bup actually said "capsize" instead of turn over and I had to ask him what that meant. Thereafter I used the word myself, as I wanted to talk salty. I heard someone else relate that a ship foundered in the inlet, but I misunderstood; later, to Brother Sammy's amusement, I told him about the ship that floundered.

During Uncle Ed's stay at Aunt Ella's cottage, he remodeled the nearest jetty. Uncle Ed had plenty of energy and liked hard work. He took the rocks from the jetty, carried them to the shore in front of the cottage and built a seawall all across the front of the lot. At each end the wall turned the corner and ran up the shore to high ground. The front wall was in the water and its wings up on dry sand. Then Uncle Ed took a wheelbarrow and shovel and dug sand from the Sound's bottom at low tide. He pushed his load of sand ashore and filled in the void behind the new seawall until Aunt Ella had a new front yard, larger than before and level from the front steps to the seawall. The rock wall was about five feet high in front and tapered in thickness from bottom to top. He finished the job in the spring. That was the year Lizzie rented Bup's cottage and the first year that Lee came with us.

The first day we arrived, Lee and I rushed down the shore to see Uncle Ed and to admire his new rock wall. Intrigued by the construction, we waded its length, examined the way Uncle Ed had fitted the various sized rocks, picked out some stone crabs, and got well splashed, our first bath of the day. We approved of the work. Lee suggested we call the edifice Fort Sumter, as it did look like a fort. Uncle Ed approved of the name and told us a ghost story in return. The fort endured all summer, but in September a hurricane howled past the island. The wind and high seas wrecked Fort Sumter and washed the sand fill away. The shore returned to its natural level. I never heard Uncle Ed comment on the fort again. Uncle Ed did not leave the mess. He removed the pile of rocks, hauled them back up the shore, and rebuilt the jetty in its original place.

From the Pamlico Inn, continuing toward Portsmouth Island, there lay a vacant stretch of shore. Only one small house, usually vacant, was near the shore. Behind it, back in the trees, were other houses. On the shore and partly in the water we discovered a round rusty boiler. It was not hard to discover the thing, for it was as big as a small house. Along the shore near it were other heavy chunks of machinery. We examined it all and concluded that a steam boat had blown up here. We told each other all about it and speculated on the cause and cost of the disaster.

We had been told that the point we could see from Cap'n Bill's dock as we looked south-west toward Portsmouth Island was called Springer's Point. Here we discovered a place of mystery, for a little way inland from the water's edge, up in the dunes and tightly wrapped in live oak trees and bushes, was a big house. It had tall gray walls, gray shingled roofs, and a gray tower sticking up through the trees. The yard was dark and shady, all the doors were locked and the windows were shuttered or dark behind the glass. We knocked cautiously on a door, ready to run but hoping somebody or some thing would open it. Nobody did. It was not like the Doxsee House, crumbling, for this one was in good repair but forbidding. If the Doxsee House was our haunted house, then this one was Count Dracula's castle, Ocracoke style. The old house was sort of scary but attractive and was the object of more expeditions than any other place, except maybe Cap'n Bill's.

Past Dracula's cottage, around the point, was another marshy place with a little stream trickling out to the Sound. Both Lizzie and Bup had told me about this place called Teach's Hole. It was where Blackbeard the pirate had been killed and his ship sunk. We liked to talk about old Blackbeard and we relished the story of his headless corpse swimming around his ship three times before it sank. We half hoped to see a headless ghost at Teach's Hole. Somehow, we never seemed to want to go there at night. It was an eerie place. One day I found an iron ball, rusty and dirty, in a sand bank near Teach's Hole. I carried it back to the cottage and proudly proclaimed it was a cannon ball from either Blackbeard's or Lt. Maynard's ship. Uncle Thomas Hill, usually a kind man, explained to me that the object was part of the speed-governing device from an old steam engine. He pointed out a rectangular slot in the ball as the place where it had been fastened to the governor. I silently rejected my uncle's explanation, although I knew it was correct, and carried the ball home with me, just in case.

While travelling on our part of the island, we usually walked along the shore. The strip of damp sand, firm and packed, just by the water's edge was the best walking. We never travelled in a straight line, though. Our normal progression was an irregular zig-zag: out in the water to investigate something, then inshore to investigate something else. When going inland we zig-zagged still following the paths and roads. All of the roads curved and wound around from house to house. If those roads had been pre-planned, then goats had been the surveyors with snakes for linesmen, or else small boys had done it.

There were lots of paths and roads, and two kinds of road surfacing. The road in front of Bup's cottage that led past Mr. Bragg's house and on down to his pier in one direction and back inland the other way, was surfaced with a dense, flat matting of wire grass, or possibly crab grass considering all the salt water nearby. This road was either a wide path or a narrow road that could just handle a flatbed truck and a pedestrian passing. The other kind of road surface, like the road that led 'round the Creek, was sand surfaced. There was also a road that ran behind Mr. Bragg's house, roughly parallel with the Sound shore, past a lot of houses and cottages and then on to the Creek before it turned along the Creek shore and joined the main sand road near a little bridge; this one alternated sand with grass. Another of the grasstops led to Springer's Point, with a branch passing the light-house and turning to sand before it crossed the beach to the ocean. On the other side of the Creek, the roads were just as curvy and crooked and often wound through oak branch tunnels. I learned I could not give strangers directions on the perfectly logical road grid system. I either had to say I did not know or offer to lead the way.

There were three general directions or geographical divisions used in travelling the island. The tip of the island on the Portsmouth end was called *Pointer Beach*. I learned that one first, as I had been there several times. The other way, and a long way off on the Hatteras end, was called *Down Below.* I had never been to Down Below. Sister had been there once in a boat with a large party of boys and girls. To my great envy, she talked a lot about the trip and picnic. Assigned a theme on her summer vacation, Sister read to her high school class her paper entitled "My Trip Down Below." She was startled at the howls of laughter her title brought. Sister, I realized in later years, had an artless innocence about some things. Sammy told people that little brother Mac sometimes had to explain things to Sister.

The third term used by the islanders was *Up Trent.* This one was vague: it was someplace in the middle of the island, but nobody ever defined it exactly for me, though I realized it represented a large, unexplored territory out there waiting for me. I tried using the term, with poor results. When I and my friends left either cottage, I was required to say where we were going. "'Round the Creek," was okay, " To Springer's Point," was acceptable, or even "Pointer Beach," but when I tried answering "Up Trent," both Aunt Lizzie and Mama called me back to explain more fully. When I finally did go on an exploration Up Trent, I did not know for sure if I was there or not.

We were allowed to go swimming in the Sound almost any time except for one hour after lunch, when a cruel and unjust ruling of our elders kept us ashore. Swimming too soon after eating was supposed to cause cramps which caused drowning. Ocean swimming was different. An ocean visit was a special group affair involving adults, a flatbed truck, and cautions about the undertow and going out too far. The surf at Ocracoke could be very rough and nobody—islanders, visitors, young or old—went swimming alone.

One early summer Sister told me she would teach me to ride the waves, as we called body surfing. I had watched the girls and their friends skidding into shore on the crest of a big wave they had jumped on out beyond the breakers. It looked like fun and

Sister was as agile as a porpoise in the surf. The two of us plunged through the breakers, swam out the right distance, and treaded water while we waited for a bigger wave. "Here it comes!" she called, "Hold on to my shoulder!" The wave was a whopper, but it broke too soon and tumbled us both, ankle over elbow, underwater. I thoroughly scrubbed the ocean's bottom all the way up the beach where the dying wave deposited me. Snorting, spitting out salt water, and wiping my eyes, I told Sister I would just as soon not ride any more waves that day. She quickly explained that that was a fluke, not wave riding. I tried again and learned to do it, but still got a tumblescrub at times.

The ocean had many moods, changing according to conditions of wind and tide. A few times stinging nettles were thick along the beach, making the ocean unswimmable. Once there were big crabs, hundreds of hard crabs, washing up in the surf. I saw them in the smooth, concave face of a just-before-breaking wave, as thick as raisins embedded in a cake. There was no swimming that day either, and nobody had brought a dipnet. Mostly, though, the ocean was fine but rough.

The strong ocean breeze blew in my face as I looked out to sea. Likewise, the breeze on the Sound side blew on me when I looked across to Portsmouth Island. I formed what I thought was a weird idea (I did not know it was a theory) that there were two winds, a sea breeze and a Sound breeze. The place where the winds met would show as a line of tangled bushes, looking pushed together, somewhere in the middle of the island. I thought about trying the two-winds idea on Mama when she fussed with me about not keeping my hair combed and parted. Mop-headed, she called it. I rejected the two-winds theory when I realized it was one wind blowing from the south and cooling both sides of the island.

The miles and miles of beach were peopled sparsely with fishermen, bathers, and shell hunters. The ocean side was all bare sand, dunes, sea oats, and wreck timbers. There were no houses on the ocean beach even in those pre-Park Service days. Nobody even thought of building a house on the ocean sands, for they had more sense and more land. Islanders and visitors alike lived in the middle of the island with the trees or on the Sound shore.

It was Sister who explained to me that the island people divided themselves into two territories. Those who lived on the lighthouse side of the island were called *Pointers*. Those who lived 'round the Creek on the other side were called *Creekers* and there was a sort of rivalry between them. Both Ella's and Bup's cottages were in Pointer territory, but summer visitors did not count. They were neither one, just summer people. Both Pointers and Creekers, other than those directly concerned with housing, feeding, or guiding visitors, did not take up a lot of time with them. The islanders were not unfriendly, they were good, polite people, but they had their own interests, and entertaining summer people was not one of them. I came to realize that there was a fourth category that was not Pointer, Creeker, nor tourist. It was the *Old Summer Visitor*. This in-between status was semi-acceptable but it took years to achieve it.

I was intrigued by the islanders' talk. They spoke of their everyday life, discussing fishing, the Sound, the tides, and their boats, all of which interested me. Their unique accent and pronunciation of words were of as much interest as their subjects. I heard one visitor at Bup's cottage explain that the Outer Banks accent was a remnant of the Elizabethan English spoken by the first settlers. I liked that idea and remembered to talk it over with Aunt Lizzie when I got home.

Aunt Lizzie disagreed with the idea—or more exactly, she did not agree with it. "We have no way of knowing exactly how the Elizabethans sounded," she said. "We can learn about their vocabularies from books of the period. We might think their polite conversations sounded coarse, because they were less restrained in the words they used than we are. But just how they pronounced words and what their accents were, we don't know. It is a pleasant thought, though."

I thought over her words and had to agree with Lizzie. I continued to enjoy hearing the Ocracokers talk, but did not try to imitate them for fear of teasing. In later years when I read articles by people claiming to know all about the Outer Banks, I realized how very right Lizzie had been. You could not catch the right sound by writing something like "hoigh toide" for high tide and make any sense of it. The Outer Banks accent has to be heard to be enjoyed. As for claiming it is Elizabethan, who has heard an Elizabethan?

I thought often of the brief conversation I heard between two Ocracoke fishermen.

"High tide yesterday," said the first one.

"High! My God! The sharks ate me collards," answered the second.

I enjoyed, too, the long salty account given by an Ocracoke lady about her recent trip to Hatteras in a gas boat. She delighted in explaining the inferiority of everything on Hatteras when compared to Ocracoke.

"I went into a caffy for a cup of coffee," she related. "When I finally got it, it were that weak you could've sighted bottom in forty fathom of it."

LIFE WITH LIZZIE

MAMA AND AUNT LIZZIE were two very different people, and I sometimes thought they did not even like each other. Aunt Lizzie considered Mama a nice young woman who lacked refinement. But, she reasoned, if this is the wife my baby brother has chosen, I will accept her and maintain amicable relations. Mama thought Aunt Lizzie was an opinionated, rigid old maid who must be placated when necessary and avoided when possible. They were both wrong, as they realized in later years.

They probably looked the parts that they imagined for each other. Aunt Lizzie was spare and reserved while Mama was plump and outgoing. They both enjoyed entertaining their friends. Lizzie liked to invite a few friends in for tea with lots of little sandwiches and sweetcakes. Mama sometimes gave a supper for the whole crowd after the square dance.

Usually their relations were cordial enough, but at times their polite phrases became frigid. My father hated these disagreements, as he loved both his wife and his sister and did not want to be a referee. I took advantage of the disagreements whenever possible. If I got into any sort of trouble at home, which happened frequently, I ran over to Aunt Lizzie's house to find sympathy and understanding—and escape punishment. If Mama was undecided about letting me do something I wanted to do, I could interject, "Lizzie didn't like the idea." Sometimes it worked.

Since the two ladies had wisely chosen different months at Ocracoke, I had the advantage of a double vacation. The days spent on the island, whether with Lizzie in June or with Mama in July, did not differ much. Both ladies realized that I would be happier and easier to control if I had a buddy with me. There were so many things for boys to do that the base of operations did not matter.

The day at either camp started fairly early with a hearty breakfast. Aunt Lizzie carried a side or two of bacon to the island, sometimes a cured ham or a shoulder, which she kept cool and shrouded in the little ventilated pantry just off the kitchen. Bacon and eggs were the usual breakfast, along with Aunt Lizzie's toast, which was thick, crisp and buttery. She had a special toaster, a four-sided tin and wire contraption that sur-rounded one burner of the Ocracoke cook stove. It was necessary to lift it off and refold it to toast the other side of the bread, but it toasted to perfection. Sometimes Lizzie varied the menu with fish instead of bacon or ham. At home she occasionally had salt cod fish for breakfast. I did not like the cod fish, but I did like the containers the fish came in, neat little wood boxes with sliding tops. Once, needing a box for something, I asked Lizzie if we could have some of that cod fish at Ocracoke, and received the cryptic answer, "Coals to Newcastle." She explained that if one wanted salt fish on the island, one ate Ocracoke corned mullets which were famous. She said that fresh fish were better and most always available.

There was a fish house out in the Sound a few hundred yards, right in front of Aunt Ella's cottage. Instead of in the Creek, which was crowded, this one was built on the edge of the channel where the owner could receive ice or fish from other

boats and repack and reship the fish. The fish-house man sometimes sold fish retail to customers in skiffs, a row-in fish house; it
was the first drive-in store I ever saw. Sometimes Aunt Lizzie
rowed out in the skiff to buy fish, and carried me along. Thus she
demonstrated that she was adept at handling small boats, one of
her previously hidden talents. Mostly, though, she ordered fish
from the owner as he passed the cottage on the way to his home.

Lunch at the cottage was a cold collation, as Aunt Lizzie took
a break from the cook stove at midday. One of the typical
Ocracoke smells, along with salt air, seaweed, fish, and myrtle
bushes, was the aroma of oil cook stove. It smelled, sometimes
smoked, and placidly gurgled. Lizzie spent some time each day
trimming and cleaning stove and lamp wicks and polishing lamp
chimneys. She was really an elegant cook, but her scope was
restricted by the oil stove. My mother was also a fine cook
though their menus were different. I might have weighed three
hundred pounds before I was sixteen if I had not expended all
that good food in constant motion!

Health was never a major problem on Ocracoke. My friends
and I, and all of the house-party members, never had a serious
illness on the island. There was no doctor at Ocracoke, but one of
the Bragg family was a very competent registered nurse. My
buddies and I never made her professional acquaintance, but we
knew her by sight and knew where she lived, up the grass road
past the lighthouse. Aunt Lizzie carried her own medicine chest,
prepared, as always, not only for our nutrition, but also for our
bodily health. She had a guaranteed cold and runny nose remedy
—three drops of turpentine on a lump of sugar, a formula seldom
needed at Ocracoke. For minor skin abrasions she relied on Witch
Hazel, and for mild interior upsets a dark brown liquid she called
"tonic."

She had other *materia medica* in her medicine chest, as I
learned the time I had the toothache. It was a bad toothache that
seized me late one afternoon. My tooth hurt so badly that I could

hardly eat any of the speckled trout Lizzie had filleted or the apple pie she had made with dried apples. The medicine chest furnished oil of cloves, which she rubbed on my gums, but to no avail. I could not sleep that night, tossing and groaning, and keeping Aunt Lizzie awake and worried. She decided on a drastic remedy and made me a hot toddy. Her formula was a table-spoonful of whiskey, a lump of brown sugar, some lemon juice, and hot water. The effect was magic. The toothache departed, I slept ten hours and awoke painfree and very pleased with myself. I had taken a drink of whiskey! That was really some-thing to tell the boys back in school. I had known what whiskey was for a long time. Daddy kept some in the top of the dining room closet. Although it smelled terrible, and was for grownups only, I had wanted to taste it. I had thought I could sample a sip some time when everybody else left home.

My buddy Billy was envious when we discussed the matter the next day. After much consultation, we both approached Aunt Lizzie just before supper and announced that we both had toothaches and wanted some of that medicine. Lizzie was momentarily shocked at our request—she was not going to encourage alcoholism. Quickly recovering her good sense, she responded, "Yes, you two scoundrels, you can have some medi-cine. Quinine is the best remedy for recurring toothaches." We knew what quinine was, and the new toothaches vanished at once.

Later that summer Billy cut his foot badly on a shell. Aunt Lizzie promptly and efficiently cleaned the cut and sat Billy in a chair on the porch with his wounded foot soaking in a Lysol solution. She told Billy that the medicine was a disinfectant; he should keep his foot in it until she returned. I had brought my puppy to the island, a little stumpy-legged rat terrier. The puppy trundled up to the pan and began to lap up the Lysol. Billy, bemused by his wound, let him drink his fill. When Lizzie came back, it was too late. She had not seen the puppy drinking, nor did Billy mention it, so she did not learn the sad details until the puppy died the next day. Wisely, she decided not to tell me the cause of the puppy's death. I did not learn of it until months later when Billy confessed. It was hard for a young scientist to admit being that dumb. The puppy had a nice funeral, though. Aunt Lizzie produced a wood box for a coffin and attended the service along with me, Billy, and two children from up the shore. The fish-house man, passing on his way home, stayed for the funeral, too.

The label on the Lysol bottle intrigued me, with its skull and crossbones and the poison warning written in red. The name seemed familiar. I asked Lizzie if it were named for that man she had read about who discovered the Mississippi River and if he had invented it. Lizzie explained that Lysol had nothing at all to do with the French explorer La Salle and that it was a different word altogether. I was never much good at French pronunciation, then or later.

After breakfast my buddies and I were free to roam, and we covered the Sound shore daily. We took a mid-morning swim either in front of the cottage or up the shore at Mr. Bragg's pier. Anywhere along the shore was good swimming.

Aunt Lizzie rarely went in swimming, but when she did she showed off another hidden talent. Some people thought "Miss Lizzie" was stern and forbidding, but they had never seen her swimming. When she donned her multi-skirted bathing suit, her high-topped bathing shoes, and her chin-strapped rubber cap that looked like an aviator's helmet, she demonstrated a side stroke that was pure Olympic. She would launch herself from the ladder on the pier, head out in a wide circle, and leave a wake like a speedboat. On regaining shallow water, she would stand up and look around with a half smile at any spectator as if to say, "Try that, you young whippersnapper!" I never saw anybody else swim like that.

I had read somewhere that ladies in olden times rode horses with something called a sidesaddle. I formed an image of a thing like a leather swivel chair in which the lady sat facing either to port or starboard with her heels drumming on the horses ribs. I imagined if the ladies learned to ride that way they were also required to swim side stroke. Mama neither swam nor rode that way. Many years later I drove Mama to visit some old friends in Hyde County where she had spent several childhood years while Bup tried cattle raising. One ancient lady, as wrinkled as a ripe persimmon, told me about Mama's riding, quoting her mother: "There comes Nita McIlhenny a-ridin' a-straddle again."

Lizzie tried to direct our interests toward things that were fun as well as educational. She started Billy and me collecting sea shells. She organized an expedition to Pointer Beach on a flatbed truck with some surf fishermen to explore and collect shells. She prevented us from collecting more than we could carry, culling our haul and keeping only perfect ones. She managed it so that we cooperated and did not think her too bossy. We built up a good collection of sand dollars, scotch bonnets, and other desirable kinds. She did not prohibit us from experimenting with those square, leathery egg cases with spikey corners. We kept them in our beds for several nights trying to incubate them and hatch little sharks or rays or whatever critters the cases contained. The experiment was not successful.

Likewise, Aunt Lizzie's attempt to interest us in a collection of birds' eggs was a failure. We managed to break almost all the eggs we carried home. Birds' eggs were not designed for transportation by small boys. Besides, the method of punching little pin holes and blowing out the contents was sickening.

Sometimes we travelled over to the ocean side with other visitors on one of the trucks. Aunt Lizzie did not care for surf bathing, but she lifeguarded while we swam. She knew something about wrecks, too, and could name a few of them. I searched the old ship timbers for something to take home. I wanted a copper spike for Bup, but I found only rusty iron ones that I could not wrench loose.

Aunt Lizzie's knowledge of what was happening each day on the island was uncanny. She did not leave the cottage all that often to go 'round the Creek or to visit people, but she knew where to join a group riding to Pointer Beach and when to meet the mailboat to pick up some packages from home.

On one memorable Saturday after Billy had gone home and before Mama came, Aunt Lizzie put on her walking shoes, picked up her parasol, and called, "Mac! Come with me. Let's go visit a place you'll like to see."

Up the Sound shore we hiked, Lizzie leading. She was tall and slender, and with her straight back she looked even taller. She could really step out. We first walked along the shore, then on the grass roads and paths, past Bup's cottage, past Cap'n Bill's, and on to Springer's Point—to visit Mr. Springer, that day in residence in Dracula's cottage. I learned that Mr. Springer and Aunt Lizzie were old friends and Mr. Springer was in no way a fearful creature of the night.

He showed us his big, old house and, in a tower room, the finest collection of sea shells I had ever seen. Mr. Springer had some large mother-of-pearl shells that were a delight to see and handle. I hoped he would give me one, but was too diffident to ask, so I did not get one.

He led us up some square-cornered winding stairs to the very top of the tower, a little window-walled room that looked across the ocean one way, and across the Sound the other. No land was visible either way. Out across the wide waters of Pamlico Sound, I was told, was Verrazzano's view. That early explorer, from the masthead of his ship, had looked across the island and gazed upon the Sound—nothing in sight but more water. He had thought he was looking at the Pacific Ocean and had so written in his log book. At least, sniffed Aunt Lizzie, Walter Raleigh's expeditions had sent in small boats to discover the mainland, and had not jumped to any such conclusions. Lizzie sounded like she had known Sir Walter well.

It was the evenings that made the month with Lizzie so very different from the month with Mama. Aunt Lizzie's story reading did it. She varied her selections after the first summer, though she still kept to the authors she had enjoyed in her school days.

She read *Gulliver's Travels* to us, a book that required a lot of pauses while she scanned ahead with a frowning face and pursed lips. Years later, I read an unexpurgated edition of Lemuel Gulliver's adventures and found out the causes of the pauses. During Lee's first visit to the island Aunt Lizzie made a false start with *Hiawatha* which we did not like, but she scored a bullseye with *Ben Hur*. We enjoyed every chapter of it, asked lots of questions, particularly about the games, and wanted more stories of ancient times.

Also of interest was the fact that the man who wrote *Ben Hur* was a Yankee general named Lew Wallace. Lee, who was Lee Wallace, disclaimed kinship with Lew. We had become interested in the Civil War, and this was Lee's field of expertise, as boats were mine and science was Billy's. The daughter of a Confederate soldier—who was born during the reconstruction era and grew up hearing war stories—might not be totally objective in relating this period of America's history: it is just possible, splendid teacher though she was, that Aunt Lizzie showed a slight Southern bias. Years later I was surprised to learn, for instance, that Lincoln was a great president and General Sherman could even be considered human.

After the first literary month with Lizzie, we added another piece of baggage to our holiday provisions. It was a big wood box which came to the store full of bolts and which Daddy altered for us. He added a hinged lid, a latch, and a rope handle on each end. We packed it full of books. It travelled in the ship's hold and was so heavy we needed help loading and unloading it.

We were reading more on our own by this time. Both of us liked to read and had begun to collect books to take to Ocracoke. Lizzie helped by collecting all the boy's books at home that had belonged to her brothers and older nephews. She started us on the G. A. Henty stories about the adventures of young English lads throughout history. We found some Tom Swift books, but considered them outdated because Tom was still fooling around with balloons and such in the age of the airplane. Among some really old books were some of the Rover Boys series, which we thought comical.

Our favorites at the time were a series about a boy named Don Sturdy. Don, a very lucky boy, had two uncles, one a big game hunter, the other a professor, who took him and his friend Teddy everywhere in the world on adventures. We did wonder sometimes how Don and Teddy got out of school so much. There seemed to be about nine hundred volumes of Don Sturdy, so we could trade them for unread ones. Mr. Appleton, the author, occasionally injected a little fun in Don and Teddy's excursions, in contrast to Mr. Henty, whose subjects were always so intent on being young British heroes that they acted a little stuffy.

Lee, who was a more sophisticated reader than I, did not share my complete devotion to Don Sturdy. Lee would some-times tease me by referring to Don Sturkeegee, or asking if I had anything new about Don Turkey. But Lee read them all, too. In fact both of us read almost anything that came within reach. One time, back home, I went around to Lee's house, and was invited to go on in by Lee's mother, who was in the front yard. As I entered I saw Lee hastily shove a book under the sofa cushion. I looked under that cushion later and discovered that Lee had been reading *The Bobbsey Twins*, one of his sister's books. I was not able to blackmail Lee over this, because Lee had caught me reading *The Red Fairy Book*. It was a satisfying thing to know, any-how.

The worst book we had ever read was called *The Wonderful Electric Elephant.* It was so bad that it held a weird fascination for us. This epic was about a boy and girl who were presented with a large electro-mechanical elephant by its dying inventor, and in this unlikely vehicle they toured the globe. We could believe in Captain Nemo's submarine or Buck Rogers' rocket ships, but *not* in electric elephants.

THE FIELD TRIP

JUST BEFORE ANOTHER SCHOOL YEAR ENDED, Lizzie and I were sitting on her front porch one evening talking about Ocracoke. Lizzie said she had engaged Ella's cottage again for June and asked me who I wanted to take with me. Would it be Billy? I was not mad with Billy any more about the puppy, so I did want to take Billy, and I asked if Lee could go too. Lizzie considered the implications of handling three boys instead of two before she answered. She had handled more than that successfully when she taught school. Besides, she liked Lee's mother very much.

"All right, Mac," she answered, "Ask them both right away so I can plan what to take."

I talked to Lee that same evening. Lee came around the next morning to say that his parents said he could go and that his mother would call Lizzie to find out what she should furnish. After Lee left, I galloped over to Billy's house and found him lying under the dining room table reading a book. Billy hollered, sure he would go. "When do we leave?" I reported to Lizzie that both Lee and Billy were going.

The plan changed the next morning. I was in Lizzie's back

yard. She was weeding her flower beds while I was filling a tulip with all the pollen I could collect from Lizzie's flowers and my Pa's vegetable garden and imagining what a gigantic strange flower would grow there next year. Billy came in the back yard and just stood there a minute before speaking. I thought he looked funny.

"I can't go," he choked out, "unless my sister Ann can go too. I'll miss her so much." Billy looked like he was about to cry.

Aunt Lizzie straightened up and looked like she was going to freeze us both. Then her expression softened and she reached over and patted Billy on the cheek. "I'm so sorry, Billy. We both wanted you to come with us. I can't be responsible for any more children, but we do want you to come. Won't you think it over some more and try not to turn us down?"

"Yes'm," Billy blubbered and turned away.

Aunt Lizzie put her tools away in the tool shed, took off her gloves and marched off, saying to me, "I'm going to see your mother."

I followed her into the house where Lizzie met Mama in the kitchen. They sat down at the table and started to drink coffee. I knew something special was going on. I also knew I would hear more if I was invisible. I trotted outside, around the kitchen and onto the old root cellar steps, which just happened to be under the right kitchen window. I was not really spying on Mama and Lizzie; I often played in the old cellar. It made a good hideout even if it did smell like rotten potatoes. I heard Lizzie telling Mama about Billy.

"The child was coerced, I'm sure, though I don't know by whom. He's a nice little fellow, and he and Mac get on well with each other. I felt so sorry for him, parroting that message. Even so, I cannot take on a thirteen-year-old girl in addition to three boys."

"Ko-hersed," I pondered. I wondered if that was another one of those darn French words. It sounded bad.

The conversation in the kitchen went on, Mama mostly agreeing with Lizzie. She said it might be a good idea to wait a few days to see if Billy, or whoever, would relent.

Mama planned even further. "I'll have a full cottage the first half of July with my regular girls and the Duffy's. Glenmore and Howard will be there, too. The last half of the month I could take Billy in with us. Let's see what happens. If he isn't allowed to go with you, I'll talk to Helen. I'll simply tell her I can take in one more guest, if he can come by himself."

The two ladies finished their coffee, Lizzie returned to her flower beds, and Mama went to the front of the house. They could agree on joint action when it was necessary for important things like Billy's problem, or how to outwit and forestall a certain female relative.

And sure enough, in mid July Billy joined the house party at Bup's cottage. I had been without a buddy since Lee had left at the end of June. Howard was too little to count and the Koonce cousins, who came too, were just girls. I was doubly glad to see Billy grinning at me from the deck of the *Russell L*.

Billy, as usual, had some big plans. He had been helping his older brother Churchill and sister Lou who were working with a lot of other young people on a museum. They were making displays and collections in an old building near the schoolhouse. They named it the Washington Field Museum, but most of the young kids called it the Bug House. Billy wanted to start a museum at Ocracoke and take it home with us. I thought it a grand idea. We began planning as we walked from Cap'n Bill's dock to the cottage. Billy stopped the museum talk long enough to say that his sister Ann had gone to visit some cousins in Greensboro since her Ocracoke plan had not worked.

I was thrilled at the thought of our own Hall of History, like the one in Raleigh. Billy intended to establish a scientific display of wildlife—stuffed, preserved, or living. Each of us would give a little, and our combined ideas grew and grew. Billy invented a name that suited both of us: *The Pamlico Biological and Historic Institute*. It would be founded right here at Ocracoke.

I accompanied Billy on the customary tour of the shore, so he could refresh his memory and inspect for changes. As we zig-zagged I explained the water shortage to Billy. No rain had fallen since early June and all the cisterns were low. The rain barrels at Bup's cottage were empty, so we would have to fill the water buckets at Mr. Bragg's hand pump. I was glad to have Billy's help, and the girls' help sometimes. The back-porch pump still furnished washing water, but my buddies and I depended on the Sound for bathing. The girls had a great big tin bathtub in their upstairs quarters, although I never understood why anybody wanted a bathtub at Ocracoke.

When we got back to the cottage all the girls petted Billy and said how glad they were to have the "Perfesser" with them. Billy grinned and preened while I fought jealousy. Mama told Billy and me she had a pile of tin cans ready for disposal. Cans were about the only garbage the house party generated and there were not many of them. Most of the groceries we bought were weighed out from bulk supplies and brought home in paper bags. There were no plastic containers. Milk bottles were return-able, and other glass jars, if large enough, were saved for canning. Little was thrown away. We carried the bag of tin cans to the back yard, pulled the old rusty shovel from under the house, beat the cans flat, and buried them. In that salty, sandy soil the cans rusted away in only a few months. The soil turned reddish-brown around the hole, and the cans returned to the earth. Everybody on the island was gentle with the environment in those days, although the word had hardly been invented.

Billy informed me that museum curators had to collect spec-imens. He had helped his brother and sister do it for the Bug House back in Washington. We started at once and caught two specimen horseturd terrapins from the Turtle Ditch and plopped them in an old lard stand with water and a brick to sit on. The turtles just sat around in the water and showed no interest in the fish head we fed them. Sister and Wookie said the poor things would die in that lard stand and prevailed upon us to release the poor specimens. As we dumped them back in the Turtle Ditch we told each other that the ditch was actually our reservoir of terrapins, which could be re-caught in time for the trip home.

We discussed other specimens. We had the previously started sea shell collection. We could add more shells and find a book like Lizzie's that showed the names of the shells. Billy said we needed to collect little creatures from the shore and water and preserve them in museum jars. We found a couple of empty peanut butter jars for a start and in the icebox we discovered a jar of sweet pickles with only a few chunks left. We ate the pickles and created another empty jar for the museum. Billy said that was not enough, but maybe we could find more along the shore. We were experienced beachcombers.

He also said we had to have some wood alcohol, or better still, some "formaldehol," to preserve the specimens in the jars. That was a serious problem, for we had no idea where to get either. We discussed using pickle juice, which seemed to preserve pickles, but that did not really seem suitable. "We'll ask 'em at the stores 'round the Creek," I suggested. Billy added, "We got to have some collecting bags, too. A sort of knapsack you sling over your shoulder."

A foraging expedition resulted in the acquisition of two burlap bags that Mr. Big Ike gave us so we would quit asking him about alcohol and formaldehol. None of the store keepers knew anything about formaldehol. The burlap bags worked fine, though. We washed them clean in the Sound, cut them down to proper size, and made shoulder straps out of the cut-off parts. We tied the parts together with fishing line. Thus equipped in the best scientific manner, we had only to select the direction of our first field trip. We would worry about formaldehol later. Billy said woods and streams were the places most favored by museum curators, and, of course, the Sound shore. I suggested the little stream that trickled out to the Sound just past Springer's Point.

After breakfast next morning we set out, knapsacks slung, dip net and gig ready, and specimen jars clanking in the bags. We caught some crabs at the first rock jetty and filled two jars. We netted some interesting looking minnows, dumped one jar of stone crabs, and put in the minnows. That left only one specimen jar in reserve. Up on the side of a sand dune, under a board, Billy discovered a peculiar looking frog. It had a large hump behind its head, growing out of its back. I thought the poor frog might have been injured or born deformed, but Billy immediately identified it as a rare "Buffalo Toad" and popped him in the last jar.

The expedition could have turned back then with all collecting jars full, but we wanted to explore further. We came to the marshy place and the little run and sat down to define our goals and objectives. Billy remembered his brother had led him up a little stream exactly like this one. That one, Billy said, began at a spring near Pioneers Bluff at home. We thought how fine it would be to discover the source of this run, and hoped it began at a spring way inland. We decided to pour out the minnows and stone crabs, easily replaceable, to free the two jars.

With collecting equipment again in order, the curators waded upstream, alert for springs and specimens. Our knapsacks were not empty. I had picked up some odd-shaped bits of driftwood, some small rocks, and shells. Billy had a vacant turtle shell, some conch eggs, and the Buffalo Toad. All sorts of little fishes and crustaceans lived in the stream, but we considered none of them worthy of collection.

I was disappointed when the source of the stream proved to be a marsh and not a spring. I had pictured a clear gush of water spouting from the side of a hill and flowing down to the Sound, and thought we might discover enough spring water to relieve the shortage of drinking water on the island. It was too far to tote it home in buckets (at least I hoped it would be considered too far) and I thought maybe Bup or Mr. Bragg and some other Ocracokers might want to run a pipeline if we discovered a spring.

But it was just a marsh, so we waded through it. It was not an open, grassy salt marsh, but more of a swamp like the ones at home. The water was dark, the stunted trees dark and spooky looking. We splashed on to a small pond with a little island in the center and a tumbled-down board shelter on the island. The pond water was deep enough to pole a skiff in, as deep as the center of the run. We waded on through it to get to the island, where we found a pile of pint bottles covered with tow bags and branches. Most of the bottles were empty, but two or three were filled with what looked like clear spring water. I picked up one to examine it just as Billy called me to look at the strange fish he had dipped up. He stumped his toe on something in the water, grappled around at the edge of the island, and found a pile of small ballast rocks. The mixture of small boys, glass bottles, and rocks could have but one result. We began to throw rocks at the pile of bottles—the crash and tinkle sounded good.

We jumped out of our tracks when a voice boomed behind us, "Don't break my bottles boys!"

We threw a startled glance around and saw a large man in high gum boots wading toward us. With no consultation, no signaling, we both took off through the swamp away from him. He did not pursue, but went instead to check his cache. We heard a cry of rage, "Gawddam ye, ye broke 'em all!"

We flew through that swamp like startled wood ducks.

The entrepreneur back on the island had exaggerated the damage. Only a few of the bottles were broken, but glass fragments covered the top of the pile of bottles and the damage looked worse than it was. He checked his main cache, a five gallon keg of the best East Lake corn whiskey that he had started to draw off in the bottles. He had quit when he heard someone coming, and he resumed bottling while he considered where to move his operation. Much later, one of my Ocracoke friends told me all about the man. He was a mainlander who reversed the usual flow of bootleg liquor, bringing his to the island for the entertainment and nourishment of visitors and islanders alike. He and his Ocracoke connections made a nice profit on their irregular trips, made when fishing was poor.

Meanwhile, Billy and I reached the inland edge of the swamp, scuttled under some myrtle bushes, and hid. We could neither hear nor see any pursuit, so we rested and whispered to each other. We still had the gig and dip net and our collecting bags. Billy said the Buffalo Toad jar was intact along with the conch eggs, but he had dropped the turtle shell. I examined my bag and reported I had lost the piece of drift wood shaped like a dinosaur. Then, feeling around deeper in my bag, I extracted the pint bottle I had been holding when Billy hollered about the fish. I unscrewed the cap, sniffed it, and passed it to Billy. The smell zinged up our eyebrows. I had a pretty good idea what it was. Rather than a toothache remedy, I told Billy it might be as good a preserving fluid as formaldehol. I put it back in the sack and we started home.

We did not know exactly where we were, as the trees and bushes were so thick. We hiked away from the swamp. It was hard to stay lost on an island with a tall lighthouse in the middle. Once we saw it through the trees, we headed for it and came out on a grass road. It proved to be the road to Mr. Springer's house, which was closed as usual. We started past the house by the shore, but stopped in alarm. The man who had yelled at us was poling a skiff along the shore. We ducked back in the bushes before he saw us, and trudged home by the long grass road. We never saw the man again.

When Mama saw us, muddy and disheveled, she asked where we had been. "A man ko-hersed us all the way through a swamp," I answered. Then I realized I had made an error in handling mothers. I had told her too much. Sure enough, Mama demanded an explanation.

"We were just looking around his fish camp and he ran us off," I answered.

Billy chimed in with, "He prob'ly thought we were goin' to mess up his camp, but we were just collectin' specimens."

"Did he actually chase you or grab you?" Mama asked.

"No'm, when we ran he just stayed at his camp."

Mama, satisfied that no violence had been intended, left us with the admonition, "Wash up for supper. You have time for a quick swim." We transferred the Buffalo Toad to our trusty museum lard stand and jumped in the Sound.

It was not until late the next morning that the curators resumed museum work. We gave the Buffalo Toad a jar lid of water and some scraps of fried fish, but he was not hungry. As we sorted out the contents of our collecting bags, Billy said we must preserve the Buffalo Toad.

"He's a rare specimen," he claimed. "We can take him home and let the Bug House display him. Churchill will fix it up for us. They can put our names on the jar. If you think it's okay let's do it."

I was willing to be famous, so we commenced to discuss our options on preservation. We had the choice of pickle juice or yesterday's find of formaldehol substitute. We opted for the substitute. We transferred the Buffalo Toad back to the jar and covered him with preserving fluid. The frog made one convulsive leap, settled back in his jar, smiled, and expired. As we tightened the jar lid and recapped the special formaldehol, we slopped a little on the floor. We were ready to collect more exhibits.

A strong odor lingered on the porch. Two young island men, strolling along the road past the cottage, slowed, sniffed, and stopped. "What are ye' doin' with that?" one asked.

"Just preservin' a frog," we answered.

"Preservin' frogs, are ye? Sweet Jesus!" With that the islanders moved on, for they had seen Mama approaching. She had been to the store and was bringing home some groceries. She mounted the front steps, stopped, wrinkled her nose as she looked around, then scowled with her eyebrows. Mama could go from happy to mad some kind of fast.

"What are you doing? What's that I smell? Who else is here?" Mama knew what she smelled. She did not allow it at the cottage, but she knew what it was. She wanted to know where it was and who had brought it. She spotted the bottle, put down the groceries, and seized it.

"Where did this come from? Answer me!" Things were getting dangerous. I gabbled an explanation that we had found the bottle yesterday and were using it to preserve a toad frog. I held up the specimen jar. "We needed some formaldehol."

"You found it, did you? And just where did you find it?"

"In the water over by Cap'n Bill's," I told her, "We just picked it up and put it in the bag."

Billy added, "I think it just washed ashore."

Mama did not connect it with the man who had chased us, and she was satisfied that nobody else had brought it to the cottage. "I've heard it called a lot of things, so I suppose formaldehol is as good a name as any. I'll take it. Do you all want a sandwich?"

The remainder of the formaldehol disappeared, but Mama did not confiscate the pickled toad. We carried him home and presented him to Billy's brother at the Bug House. There was no record of any other pickled Buffalo Toad in any other museum. We were pleased to have contributed something to scientific knowledge.

THE MONTH WITH MAMA

BUP'S COTTAGE WAS BIGGER THAN ELLA'S and it needed to be, for Mama took a big house party with her. The main purpose of the trip to the island was to provide a summer vacation for Sister and her friends, six to eight girls in their mid to late teens.

I went along as an appendage to the group. I enjoyed the atmosphere of gaiety and frivolity of these (to me) nearly grown-up girls, and had alternate seizures of puppy love for them. In turn I had crushes on Wookie, Cousin Helene, Wookie again, Mary Lee, and Evelyn, especially Evelyn, and the others.

Mama volunteered to superintend the girls because she loved staying at Ocracoke and she enjoyed the house party as much as the girls. She was determined to enforce her own rules of hours and habits on her group and on visitors alike. The girls were biddable; they were as high-spirited as most teenagers, but not wild.

Mama's strongest commandment was the prohibition of drinking by residents and guests. She was strict about this, and several young, male visitors were sent away with reddened ears and numbed feelings because Mama suspected they had imbibed spirits. Mama was not so intent on law enforcement during this era of national prohibition as she was on good behavior enforcement around her girls. She was not a teetotaler at home, as she would have her glass of wine on birthdays and family dinners and a glass of egg nog at Christmas, but on Ocracoke she was as dry as a dune top.

With all those girls, boys appeared, both islanders and summer visitors. Mama welcomed them all if they kept the rules. There were weekend visitors, mid-week visitors, and sometimes overnight visitors. There were Washingtonians, Belhavenites, and Pantegonians, besides the Ocracokers and others from far away places. The young men stayed at Cap'n Bill's, at other cottages, or camped on the beach. Occasionally Mama would let some of them stay overnight in one of the porch rooms, but these were usually occupied by visiting kin folk, for both my mother and father had lots of brothers and sisters who all liked the island, and came for a week or a weekend.

Sister and the girls always used the two upstairs rooms. Mama used the downstairs bedroom off the living room, while my buddies and I were mobile. We used the little back room, the porch rooms, a corner of Mama's room, or even the kitchen, all depending on how many migratory relatives showed up. I slept on a folding canvas-and-stick camp bed that they called an army cot. I thought it was pretty grand to have my own army cot, and it was easy to clean it up on those occasions when too many cool drinks caused my bladder to founder in the night. I hated this failing and tried to conceal it by mopping and washing up the signs before anybody else saw them. I assumed a belligerent nonchalance about it—also a failure.

On one of those rare nights when the breeze failed and the mosquitos came boiling out of the bushes, avid for blood, two of the Pantegonians were camping out. They looked so pitiful that Mama let them use a porch room. When asked how it was sleeping in the tent, the one called Little Bud answered, "Well, ever time I turned over I squashed so many mosquitos, it sounded like a mule chompin' apples."

For a part of the month the house party at Bup's cottage included a very special family member. This was Mary Young, Mama's colored cook. Her skin was a rich chocolate color. She was of medium height, plump, with a round face made for smiling. Her large, brown eyes were expressive: she put more humor in the way she rolled them than in the loudest laughter. Always neat in dress, neither the hottest kitchen, nor the biggest meal ever disarranged her. She was not, definitely not, a mere employee. She was my former nurse, our cook and housekeeper for many years, and Mama's second in command. When Mama was away Mary Young was the boss; the girls and I, and visitors too, knew it. If she worked at it, she could assume a formidable scowl to reinforce her instructions if she thought it necessary, but I knew she was as malleable inside as Aunt Lizzie, most of the time.

Mary Young had no children of her own, but she had raised several orphaned nieces and nephews and later helped raise their children. She did more than provide food and shelter for her wards. She enrolled them in the parochial school and found the money for music and band lessons, or any other extra activity she thought was good for children. Mary Young loved all children. Though I was one of a series of children in her care, she sometimes referred to me as her "guardian child." I was lucky.

Mary Young, however, did not like to be bothered by anyone when she was busy in the kitchen. Whenever my buddies or I wanted a between-meals handout—which was between all meals—we asked Mary Young. She would sometimes greet us with her scowl and answer, "Don't come penetratin' through my kitchen," or "I'm too busy fixin' supper. I ain't stud'in' you." Then we got the snack and a big smile. Real displeasure, which she seldom showed, was expressed by silence or monosyllables.

She did not enjoy beach activities: she neither fished nor swam. She visited the Bryants, her black friends on the island, but mostly she relaxed by sitting in her rocking chair on the porch to enjoy the breeze and the girls' conversation. When necessary

she cut through the girls' chatter with her common sense comments, "Finish yo' supper before you do that," or "Put on yo'
hat—the sun's still hot."

Some of Mary Young's comments were as hilarious as they
are hard to recapture. Her description of one old gentleman,
wearing a suit, high-topped shoes and collar, who wiggled and
twisted as he talked and asked lots of questions, was, "Preacher
wid the fleas." She predicted President Roosevelt's re-election
(she called him something like Rosybell) by stating, "They's fifteen children named Franklin D. in my neighborhood. Ain't a
one named Wendell."

Her best efforts were often used in practicing "one-upman-
ship" on Mama. In later years Mama became a bird watcher, so
Mary Young did too. Once Mama commented on the scarcity of
bluebirds. Mary Young said, "I see lots of bluebirds." Mama disagreed. They were both working on something in the kitchen at
home that afternoon when Mary Young called Mama's attention
to a large, sassy blue jay in a bush outside the window.

"That's not a bluebird," said Mama, "That's a jay."

"He's a bird, ain't he? He's blue ain't he?"

Mama had to answer "yes" to both questions.

"Well then!" Mary Young concluded.

In the face of this unanswerable logic, Mama retired to the
living room. Mary Young, I saw, smiled broadly to herself as she
continued working.

Mary Young came to the island to be with us, but she did not
stay the whole month. Two weeks was her limit to stay away
from her husband Capus. She returned in mid-month, never
enjoying the boat trip. She sat in that stuffy cabin, never seasick,
upright and stolid, unmoving, a monument to endurance, love,
and good behavior.

The food at Bup's cottage did not vary much from that served by
Lizzie, but the quantities prepared were vast. Besides Mama,

Mary Young, the girls, me, and my buddy, there were usually visiting relatives or extra guests. It became almost a custom for some of the other house parties from home going to nearby cottages, to take breakfast at Bup's as soon as they got off the boat. I never heard anybody say, but they must have arranged it ahead. Sometimes a half-dozen extras came for an early breakfast on Sunday or Thursday morning. Those breakfasts were not strictly bacon and egg affairs, although those items were served. Fresh fish often appeared on the breakfast table and fried chicken, hot or cold. Biscuits or cornbread accompanied the toast, and gallons of coffee.

All this food would have been too much for one oil cookstove, but Bup's cottage had two pieces of kitchen equipment that Ella's lacked. First was the big, black wood range. This monster had six or eight eyes on the top and a big oven underneath. That wood range had a mind of its own. It obeyed Mary Young absolutely, Mama most of the time, but for other cooks it was too hot or too cold just as it chose. Not many people could outsmart that wood stove; the others cooked on the oil stove. Under any cook's ministrations the wood range warmed the kitchen considerably more than was needed in July.

There was a moderate-sized icebox in the kitchen, like Aunt Ella's, but on the back porch was another monster. Bup had built an icebox that was big enough for a sizable house party. He had built it of good tongue-and-groove juniper, an inner and an outer shell, filled in between with slabs of cork. It was lined with shiny zinc sheets and divided into two compartments. It had two heavy hinged tops, sometimes pulled open with a rope and pulley. It looked like a coffin without the handles, though it was bigger than a coffin. At the left end—where the feet would be—was the ice compartment that held one of the hundred-pound blocks brought down by the Washington boat and delivered by skiff. (A lot of iced tea was drunk at Ocracoke). At the other end—the head end—were the racks for the eggs, butter, meat, fish and vegetables that kept the house party well fed. Two boys could have slept in that icebox.

Aunt Lizzie bought fresh vegetables from the stores 'round the Creek or from island gardeners. The islanders raised enough for their own needs with some surplus for others, but not enough for all the summer people. Pa kept the house party supplied from his garden. I enjoyed meeting the boat and helping to unload the crates and bushel baskets of corn, okra, tomatoes, string beans, butter beans, cabbage, carrots, and peas. The girls' parents would often send watermelons and cantalopes, and from one mother came tall, square chocolate cakes. Some chickens were raised on the island and some were shipped in.

The Ocracoke fishermen brought in the best seafood in the world, all kinds of fish in all sizes, from frying size to the great big channel bass called drum. Mary Young liked to roast drum in the woodstove oven with stuffing, onions, potatoes, and gravy. Oysters, clams, and scallops all came to the table, as well as crabs, both hard and the rarer soft-shell crabs.

Once I discovered a lot of clams right beside the pier near the cottage. I dug up all I could carry, proudly brought them home, and was depositing them on the kitchen table when Mama turned me right around. She sent me back to the shore to redeposit my clams on the Sound bottom. I had raided, in ignorance, Mr. Bragg's ready bed where he kept the clams he had dug elsewhere until Miss Lena was ready to serve them to their guests.

One elderly female cousin of parsimonious persuasion once did the same thing, but declined to return them when the matter was explained to her. "Finders keepers," she smirked, but she soon found she had stronger forces to contend with than her own acquisitive instinct. Aunt Lizzie, who was visiting briefly, and Mama exchanged an understanding glance. Those two could practically read each other's mind, though they did not always enjoy what they read. While Mama beckoned to her cousin, "Come out here for a little chat," Aunt Lizzie, without further discussion, returned the clams to their owner's bed.

The house party rarely ate beef or pork, for with no refrigeration in the boats or stores it could not be shipped in, and only a few of the Ocracokers raised pigs or cattle. Sometimes, though, an island farmer slaughtered a yearling and sold what fresh beef his own kin did not need. The beef sold for twenty-five cents a pound, whatever the cut. Mama and Lizzie did buy some beef but mostly stocked the kitchen with prime fresh fish and chicken. The stores carried a full stock of canned goods and staples such as flour, sugar, and cornmeal. The only grocery-store foods that sometimes ran out between boats were fresh milk and bread, but that caused no hardship. Canned milk would do as a substitute, while biscuits and cornbread would outdo the "light" bread from the store. Though the woodstove operators might demur, everybody preferred home-baked bread.

After those big breakfasts and before a big supper, everybody ate a light lunch. Sandwiches were the menu, and each made his own. We favored peanut butter and jam, sometimes baloney. With several "sam'witches," a piece of cheese, and iced tea, we hung on until suppertime.

There were more people our own age in the vicinity of Bup's cottage than at Aunt Ella's. All of the children dressed alike, the islanders favoring long pants instead of shorts. I had never heard of blue jeans, calling them overall pants, which was what Doss wore. The Ocracokers wore baseball caps instead of the lose-able straw hats issued to us.

We became friends with the Bragg grandchildren, Doss and Jeff. I had known Doss from the first summer but it was not until the next year, while we were off on an important exploration of the woods behind the Nunnelee house, that I learned an important fact about her. Doss started back in the thick bushes and,

turning to me, motioned for me to wait. "Mac, you stay here."
On returning she added, "I had to make me water." That was
when I found out she was a girl. It did not matter very much that
she was a girl, for she knew all the island's paths and trails and
was the leader on many expeditions.

Our reading was expanded by the discovery of the Braggs'
library. Miss Lena had a great big glass-fronted bookcase holding
several shelves of books under maximum security. She let the
young folks read these in the house but not take them away. Billy
and I looked through all the titles, but were not much interested
in the set of encyclopedias, the novels, nor the *Proceedings of the
South Georgia Methodist Convocation of 1903.* On searching the
bookcase more carefully, however, we discovered a real gem—a
thick home medical book, designed to cure or kill a patient if no
doctor was available to do so. Miss Lena was doubtful about letting
us have this one, but she finally allowed us to look at it on the
floor in front of the bookcase under her intermittent observation.

We passed over the colorful illustrations of compound frac-
tures and chicken pox rashes, to light on several pages of lurid
pictures of cancers, tumors, and ulcers. Billy, the science consultant,
said this last one was pronounced "use-alers," and was a sort of
big sore. We were entranced by all those strange horrid shapes.
For a while, instead of forts, castles, and canals in the sand, we
modeled cancers and tumors. I artfully built a "use-aler" of yellow and red sand, blue clay, and green seaweed that all agreed
looked just like the picture. Fortunately, this phase soon passed.

The only exceptions to Mama's no-drinking rule were her sister
Margaret and her husband. Aunt Margaret and Uncle Thomas
Hill liked a highball before supper. They did not flaunt their
habit and usually had their drinks in their room or in the kitchen.
Aunt Margaret was Mama's closest sister in age and affection.
They liked to do the same things, but never agreed how to do
them. They could have identical goals and objectives, but different

ways, means, and methods. They liked to give parties together, but not to work together to produce the parties.

One year the two sisters decided to have a supper party after the square dance. They agreed on the kind of party and the refreshments, and disagreed on details. Mama was a meticulous party planner, wanting each step laid out ahead and each detail of preparation assigned to somebody. After the basic plan was set, Aunt Margaret's method was to have each person involved select his own part and carry it out however he pleased. It was one way or the other (Prussian General Staff method versus British Muddling Through). Surprisingly, both ways worked, although Aunt Margaret's was often more fun.

In this instance, Mama's plan was for her to make the potato salad that afternoon while Aunt Margaret readied the four chickens, with some of the girls helping. Sister was to go to the store for bread, cheese, mayonnaise, and things. Someone was assigned tea and coffee and someone else a green salad. Mama said she would leave the pavilion early to fry the chickens and set the table with whoever was available, meaning me if I could not escape.

Aunt Margaret agreed to the chicken detail and increased the number to six, as she thought she might invite a few extra people. She bought the chickens and sought out two of the young Ocracokers who sometimes came to the cottage.

"Boys," she said,"how about dressing these chickens for me? I'll pay you, and then you come help us eat them tonight after the dance."

The islanders, not liking the term "dressing the chickens," feigned misunderstanding, "Lord, Miss Margaret, we can't dress 'em, but we'll pick 'em and gut 'em for ye if that'll help." They took the chickens with them and delivered them back to the cottage in good time, picked, gutted, cleaned, and dressed in modest little brown paper skirts. Aunt Margaret congratulated the two islanders that night on bringing the best-dressed chickens she had ever seen.

Aunt Margaret went visiting then, after leaving the message that she would bring home the bread, mayonnaise, cheese, and some pickles from the store. Mama spent the afternoon with potato salad and planning. Aunt Margaret returned as scheduled, enlisted some of the girls, made a mound of sandwiches, and set the table. Everyone ate a light supper before going to the pavilion.

Mama returned early to fry the chickens. Aunt Margaret came back a little before party time, bringing two well-dressed strangers into the kitchen. "Nita, I've brought two new fry cooks. We'll finish here. You go outside and cool off." But Mama stayed until the chickens were fried because she felt she had to superintend the new cooks. She became hotter and hotter, and more and more annoyed with Margaret. When finally Margaret and the new fry cooks had carried all the food to the big table in the front room, Mama marched out to the porch to cool off and smoke a cigarette.

As she was leaving the kitchen, still another new guest arrived to join the throng, a visitor Aunt Margaret had met at another cottage, a Judge Somebody. Mama, cool and comfortable again, decided to stay outside awhile longer and listen to the clatter of people enjoying themselves. The judge, having finished his refreshments, walked out on the porch to light his cigar. Discovering the woman he had seen leaving the kitchen, and being a suave gentleman, he stepped over to her and commented politely, "That was a very good supper you prepared, and I want to thank you. Are you a native or did they bring you with them?"

Mama's frustration boiled over. She flared at him, "Well, you are a damn fool!" and stalked off to her room.

Mystified, the judge reported to Aunt Margaret, "It seems I've insulted your cook, though I don't quite understand what I did wrong." He was annoyed, too. He was not used to being called a damn fool when he was just trying to be polite.

Aunt Margaret was much amused. "That was no cook. That was the matriarch." Then she went to get Mama and smooth things over. Mama smiled forgiveness and re-welcomed the judge. His feathers still seemed a little ruffled, but he came from a long way off, and there was little chance that any of us would ever appear in his court.

Mama worried planning the party, Aunt Margaret enjoyed preparing it, and the whole crowd enjoyed attending it. As Mary Young said, "There's more'n one way to skin a cat."

I added one feature to Bup's cottage that other houses did not have—the shipyard developed around the corner of one side porch. I had begun to learn woodwork from both Pa and Bup, and naturally began to make boats. I brought my tool chest to Ocracoke, and with Lee as co-owner, founded the Ocracoke Shipyard. It was actually a few boxes of tools and supplies stacked against the wall, with some boards stuck under the porch. When the shipyard was operating it covered a sizable section of porch.

The supply of timber for the yard came from boards found around the cottage and washed up on the shore. Barrel staves from the beach made splendid hulls for low-lying Civil War rams and ironclads. Lee was chief designer of these because of his knowledge of the period. The shipyard turned out several *Merrimac*s before constructing a *Monitor*. The *Merrimac* (Lee did sometimes remember to say *Virginia,* the ship's correct name) always won the sea battles they fought by ramming. We wanted to make cannons, but scorned wooden ones, and found nothing suitable for gun barrels on the beach or under the house.

Sail boats were my specialty. I made a replica of the *Russell L.,* with sails cut from a torn pillow case Mama furnished. It sailed well, but was lost at sea on an outgoing tide. Our favorite craft were a pair of Viking longships with whittled dragons on their bows and rows of bottle caps for shields along the sides. They sailed well, but the shipyard was almost forced out of business because of those Viking ships. Mama recognized one of her striped dish towels in the two mainsails. The dish towel had mysteriously fallen off the clothesline and into the shipyard's stores. I had to cross-my-heart promise not to do that again.

A shortage of timber also threatened the shipyard with ruin, but a letter home to Pa filled the need. When I met the Washington boat the next week I was pleased to receive a personal freight shipment. It was a large white pine box with my name painted on it, so heavy that we could just carry it back to the cottage. Inside the box were more white pine boards and several bags of nails. (Hardware stores got lots of stuff shipped in white pine boxes in those days.) Anyhow, the shipyard was back in business.

Uncle Thomas Hill contributed to the shipyard's success after he saw me using the draw knife as a "push" knife on a board wedged against a porch column. The yard possessed no vise. Uncle Thomas Hill went 'round the Creek and bought several short oak boards, a heavy hinge, some screws, and a long bolt with a wing nut. He proceeded to construct a clamp that he fastened to the porch column at the edge of the porch. It worked so well that I felt obliged to tell everybody what my uncle had invented. Uncle Thomas Hill modestly murmured that he really did not invent the screw clamp. Aunt Margaret pinched his cheek and claimed, "My Toddy Mouse can invent anything." I thought that was a sissy name for such a nice man.

I became more conscious of the house-party girls that summer. I had enjoyed listening to their chatter at times, and began to want to attract their attention to me. I did not understand just why I felt this way. As a result, my behavior around Sister and the girls became particularly obnoxious. I released two hard crabs in the girls' bedroom. The crabs scuttled under a bed, but came out when the girls went up to change into bathing suits. Their shrieks of dismay (the girls' not the crabs') were most satisfying to me. I inserted jelly fish in some shoes left on the porch to dry. The owner's disgust was most rewarding. What the girls did not understand was that these pranks were tokens of juvenile male admiration.

My most atrocious behavior, though, was directed toward Sister and her new boy friend. His name was Baxter and his family had a house 'round the Creek. He was a pleasant young man, approved by Mama, liked by the rest of the girls, and particularly liked by me, for Baxter had the use of a sail skiff. I began to follow Sister and Baxter when they walked around together, never dreaming that they might prefer to be alone. Sister usually tolerated me, but she worried about what I might say, because Brother Sammy had invented a nickname for Baxter.

It was a mean nickname. Baxter possessed a prominent nose. It was really no bigger than Sammy's nose and it was not as big as the eagle-beak carried around by one of the island clans, but it stayed sunburned a fiery red all summer. Sammy had named him "Bloomer Nose." My buddies and I thought this was the most hilarious nickname ever, with its recognition of the blooming red color and its connotation of mysterious girls underwear. We giggled whenever we heard it and said it to each other. Sister was not going to allow Baxter's feelings to be hurt, so she enlisted Mama's help in making me shut up. I did stop saying it most of the time. I also realized that the hanging threat of saying it was just as teasing as the actual deed. It was most unusual for me to displease Sister on purpose, so my meted punishment was as just as it was swift.

Sister and Charlotte walked over to Cap'n Bill's that afternoon, with me tracking them. They strolled past the pavilion and out to the end of the dock. I happened to turn around and saw Baxter emerging from the pavilion.

"Here comes old Bloomer Nose," I chortled.

There was an instant reaction from the girls. Sister was

impelled by embarrasment for Baxter, and Charlotte, remembering the jelly fish in her shoes, seized the fleeting opportunity of
having Sister as an ally in punishing the brat. They grabbed me,
arms and legs, and threw me off the dock. The first thing I saw
when I popped to the surface was Sister's anxious face peering
down at me. She was ready to jump in to rescue me, but that was
not necessary at all. I had long ago progressed past the dog-paddle
and was a good swimmer with a strong overhand stroke that I
said was the Australian Crawl. Any danger of drowning was as
remote as the chance of being swallowed, like Jonah, by a whale.
I swam quickly around the dock and into shallow water, with
Sister, Charlotte, and Baxter tracking me from up top. I stood up
in shallow water, red-faced and spitting with rage. The girls and
Baxter had vanished when I got ashore. The girls sent Mama a
message that they were having supper at another cottage and
would be home later.

I could not stay mad at Sister very long, and forgave her by
suppertime. I stayed mad with Charlotte, instead, for two or
three days, until she got a huge watermelon on the Washington
boat. I decided that day I had punished Charlotte enough and
allowed her to give me a slice of the watermelon. I did not say
"Bloomer Nose" again.

THE PERFECT OPPORTUNITY

OCRACOKE WAS PROBABLY THE SAFEST PLACE for children in the State, excepting the hazards of sea and Sound. I could not remember when I learned to swim and thought I probably was born knowing how. My earliest recollection was the time I fell off the pier at Uncle Fred's cottage at Pamlico Beach. I remember the delighted feeling of sitting in the shallow water while everybody else was jumping in around me.

At home my elders had started drilling operations about the growing hazard of automobile accidents, but that hardly existed on the island. There were few vehicles on the island in those days. I had heard of only one incident at Ocracoke. Two of the island's young men had a head-on collision on the ocean beach speedway. They were playing chicken and neither one would give in. They survived; their trucks did not.

Elizabeth O'Neal, an Ocracoke friend a few years older than Sister, told me about cars at Ocracoke when she was a little girl. A ride in a car, she said, was more push than ride until people learned how to negotiate the soft sand. Her father, Mr. Big Ike, bought the first one, a Model T Ford. Then Captain Dave

Williams bought one, followed by his cousin Dallas Williams, who bought the third Model T. A little later Cap'n Bill Gaskill bought the first truck. When a neighbor asked if it was a Ford, Cap'n Bill answered, "It's all I can A-Ford." None of the vehicles had licenses until years later when the state began to build roads on the island.

At home in Washington on hot August afternoons, I suffered withdrawal symptoms when I would have been swimming had I been at Ocracoke. There were no good places to swim within easy walking distance. The river bottom was muddy close to town and I was forbidden to swim from the docks in town (and had to do so on the sly). I had been spoiled by the wide beaches and the cool green waters of the island. The closest good place was Bup's farm where the Koonce cousins lived, and to get to that nice beach required a ride. Mama, Sister, and Sammy drove the old Star automobile after Pa got a new one. Sister and Sammy loved to drive, but were restricted in scope. Mama did not like driving, but did at times, and liked to visit her sister, Aunt Libby, at the farm. Nagging her to go swimming did not work, so I tried a persistent, calm appeal for swimming as a necessity for health, cleanliness, happiness, or whatever else I could invent. My method worked if Mama wanted to see Libby that day.

One afternoon, she announced she would drive to the farm, and she told me I could ask Billy. She told us to put on our bathing suits, bundle our clothes and towels, and be ready in ten minutes. I stumped upstairs to put on my suit, suddenly reluctant to go. My bathing suit was to blame: it was a new one to replace my old moth-riddled, rock-snagged grey one—and it was bright red. I suspected it was a girl's bathing suit and hated it at first sight. "Nonsense," Mama said, "It's a boy's suit."

I was not convinced, because the only time I had worn it, a man said, "Hey little girl." But I put it on, lured by the thought of swimming.

When I rejoined Mama, she handed me a quarter to buy two

boxes of cakes for the outing. She told me to get one of vanilla wafers and one of my favorite, "fig-newts." Mr. Powell's A & P store was just around the corner on Market Street. I objected to going in my bathing suit. Mama began to lose patience.

Cousin Betsy had told me about bathing suits only the week before when we were all at Bup's house. Betsy was older, and often instructed the younger cousins in customs and procedures. She had said that it was against the law to wear a bathing suit on the street. Furthermore, she told us that a policeman would arrest anyone he saw downtown in a bathing suit. I tried to explain this. Mama told me again, "Nonsense. There's no such law." I was worried that my cousin might know more law than my mother: Betsy knew all the latest news and had a very positive manner.

I realized I had serious problems. There was no other store close by and the A & P store was right across the street from the Police Station. Here I was, forced to violate the law while wearing a girl's bathing suit. I decided my only hope was speed. I would run in and out of the store so fast that no policeman could catch me, and, hopefully, no one would recognize me.

I marched down the front steps, took a good ready, then dashed out in the street—right in front of a pick-up truck. The driver could not avoid me. He squalled his tires, the girls in the truck screamed, and truck and boy thudded together. I had actually run into the truck. I was knocked down and disappeared under the vehicle.

The two girls stumbled from the truck, still screaming. The white-faced driver ran to me stretched out behind his truck, lying between the tire marks. I lay still, my head bloody. Mama ejected from the front door, raced out in the street and knelt by me. Calling up her nursing experience, she determined I was not dead. Miss Pat, a neighbor, ran out, followed by others. Mama asked Miss Pat to call Daddy and then bring a basin of water and a towel. The driver, staggering and stammering, tried to explain what happened. He kept pulling one hand through the other as if he wanted to detach his fingers. Mama sent him after Miss Pat to bring a blanket. She washed my oozing head where I had been half scalped by something under the truck. She realized the wheels had not run over me. I began to wiggle and groan.

Just as Pa drove up, a policeman came around the corner to help. He had come to investigate a reported accident, *not* to make a bathing suit arrest (thus proving who knew the most law). He helped Daddy wrap me in the blanket and place me in the back seat of the car. Somebody had called Dr. Rodman for Mama, so we drove to meet him at the hospital. Miss Pat treated the driver and his passengers for shock. Billy stood by to tell latecomers all about the accident.

I awoke on a rolling table at the hospital. I felt a stinging-burning on the side of my head where Dr. Rodman had cleaned the wound. I was covered by a sheet and was content to lie there while Dr. Rodman and a pretty nurse bandaged my head. Mama had sent for my clothes and helped me dress. I sat up then and asked who had the quarter and could we get the sweet cakes and go on to the farm. They took me home instead. I never saw that hateful red bathing suit again.

Mama put me in the spare bedroom, bigger than my own, for Dr. Rodman had ordered a week of bedrest and observation. I enjoyed every minute of my convalescence. I lay propped up in bed, the center of attention, waited on by everybody. Mama was my head nurse, assisted and overseen by Lizzie. Sister came home early from a visit with Cousin Helene to take her turn at nursing, Pa sat with me in the evening, and Bup stopped by daily. Sammy visited at times as did other relatives.

Mama brought the little bell from the dining table, the one I was forbidden to touch. She instructed me to tinkle it if I needed something when nobody was in the room. I jangled that bell to have my pillows adjusted, to have a window shade altered, to get another book, or to ask for a fresh glass of water. The little bell disappeared after the second day.

I did not know that poor, sick invalids were supposed to have delicate appetites. I ate three meals a day and in between gorged on ice cream with ginger ale poured over it. Mary Young made me a chocolate cake and Lizzie made a "Devil Cake." The man who was driving the truck sent me a present—a big toy steam shovel, which was placed in the room to be admired. I was almost ready to recommend being run over to my buddies.

Brother Sammy seemed particularly concerned one night and asked me if there was anything I wanted. I recognized this opportunity and seized it. There was a model ship stored away on a shelf in an upstairs closet, something that I had coveted since I first discovered it. The ship belonged to Sammy who was too old to play with toy boats, but had flat refused to give it up, however many times I asked.

"Yeah," I answered, "How about that ole boat in the closet?"

Sammy sighed and left the room, mumbling to himself. He returned a few minutes later bearing the torpedo boat, which he laid on the foot of the bed. I thanked him and groaned a little to keep from grinning.

The torpedo boat came to Ocracoke the next summer. It was a handsome boat model, with a high flared bow, cabins, pilot house, and smoke stack. It spat wooden torpedos from a spring-loaded tube in the bow. Best of all, it had a powerful clockwork engine geared to a propeller and would speed through the water for a short distance. The engine was equipped with a key stuck in a socket behind the pilot house, to wind the engine. The socket leaked. The little boat leaped through the water, throwing minia-ture sheets of spray and dripping salt water on the engine. It was designed for quiet ponds, not rough sounds. I learned to upend the boat after use to drain the water, but did not realize what corrosion was doing in the engine room. I was too carefree to ask questions about maintenance. The engine quit, so I put it aside until I went home. When I asked Pa for help, we removed the deckhouse to see the red ruin of an engine—a mass of rust. Even so, I thought, the boat had been worth a little blood in the street.

Sammy may have been too old to play with toy boats, but I was too young and too feather-brained to take care of them. I could have asked Pa, or Bup, or Sammy what to do with a wet marine engine sooner than I did, or I could have asked someone at the cottage like Uncle Thomas Hill for help. I was not the expert in many things in 1932 that I became a couple of years later.

The accident had no lasting effect on me, but it did on Mama. She began to give me the same instruction every time I left the house, "Look both ways before you cross the street!" She said it all through my school years. She did not realize how galling it was to be told how to cross the street when I was sixteen and escorting a girl. She even said it on the day I left home to attend World War II. She said it everywhere except Ocracoke.

The first July after the accident, as I dashed out of the cottage to jump in the Sound for my first swim, she started, "Look both— "

I stopped and looked at her as did the girls.

She modified it, "Look both ways for sharks and sea noddies!"

FAUNA & FLORA

"AND WHAT ARE THE CHIEF FORMS OF WILDLIFE on these islands now?"

This was the question put to Mama by one of her visiting cousins. He was wearing a hot-looking black suit, but I do not remember his name. He looked like a Sunday-school superintendent and he talked like one, too, as he droned on at Mama as they sat on the front porch. I was around on the side porch watching Bill Ballance install a new window sash. This was the same Mr. Ballance who owned the well with the extra good water and the billy-goat guard. Grandpa had written Mr. Ballance about the window.

When we heard the Sunday-school superintendent ask Mama about local wildlife, Bill Ballance answered at once, "Summer people!" He winked at me. They did not hear him on the front porch, so Mama started to tell the superintendent about the Banker ponies. I did not agree with either answer but liked Mr. Ballance's version best.

The ponies were the most publicized of the island's wild creatures. I had seen them at a distance, flickering behind a sand dune, or a few of them galloping way down the beach. I had gone to a Fourth of July round-up where the new colts were captured, marked, and released. There I saw people, horses, cars, and flat-bed trucks in a distant jumble, though the round-up was over before I got there. When I asked where the horses came from, somebody told me that their ancestors were ship-wrecked Arabian horses. That was of more interest.

I had discovered a new building project off behind the head of the Creek—a dance hall and some other things—where a man named Mr. Wahab, Mama said, was doing the work. Brother Sammy told me that Mr. Wahab was an Arab who washed ashore with the horses. Or rather his grandfather did, Sammy amended. Now *that* was an interesting idea, until Sister pointed out Mr. Wahab to me. He was dressed like the other men on the island and not in the long robes and funny head gear that Arabs in pictures wore. I was disappointed in the loss of the tale of a ship-wrecked Arab.

To me and my friends the most impressive of the island's wildlife were not the horses nor the summer people, but the geese. The geese roamed the island in groups of twenty or so. I did not know how many geese there were total, for I had only seen two of their flocks at the same time, but I had seen them all over the island. The geese all looked alike, so I never knew whether I had seen forty or four hundred of them. Nobody I asked could tell me how many there were.

They were unemployed geese who formerly worked as live decoys for hunting guides. Their wings had been clipped and they could not fly. The law on goose hunting had been changed and the use of live decoys was no longer legal. Hence the geese all lost their jobs. Perhaps that was why they were so disgruntled and so ill tempered. Being jobless had not affected their lives very much. They foraged up and down the shore, living well on green sprouts, beach peas, bugs, and small sea foods. Those geese did not waddle; they swaggered. They owned the stretch of island they occupied. Aunt Lizzie said the proper term for a herd of geese was *gaggle*. For once Aunt Lizzie was wrong. They went in *gangs* like big city street gangs of later years. And they were mean. If we bothered them too much, the old geese and ganders would charge, with beaks open, necks out-thrust, hissing and flapping their stumpy wings. Wise boys retreated.

Sister had told me about Brother Sammy and Cousin Tommy's unfortunate encounter: they had been careless while teasing the geese one time and the gang caught them, knocked them down, and swarmed all over them, biting, pecking, and beating with their bony wing tips. Uncle Joe witnessed the battle and shooed the geese off before the boys were injured. The story interested me, so I asked Mama about it later, just to hear it again. I was smart enough not to laugh, and tried to look sad and worried about it. It was too bad that Sammy and Tommy got beat up, but as long as it had to happen, I wished I could have seen it.

My buddies and I avoided the geese most of the time, only occasionally throwing a shell at them and running. Once, though, the geese did us a great favor. Neither Lee nor Billy was there, but that week I had met a boy named Bernard who was staying at the Pamlico Inn.

Cap'n Bill, in one of his rare jovial moods, had given us each a co'cola. We were rared back on a bench in the pavilion that afternoon surveying the Sound and scenes, and guzzling our drinks when we were introduced to John Jay. We had seen him before and avoided him, for he was a sneering, fat fourteen year old. I had seen him previously at home, all dressed up for Sunday School, which was understandable, but John Jay topped off his Sunday suit with a little man's hat. I hated him for that hat, and now John Jay had come to Ocracoke and was staying at the Pamlico Inn with his folks.

John Jay spotted us first and crept up behind us. He wrapped his arm around each of our necks in turn and, holding our heads under his own arm, gave us what he called a scalp massage—a hard knuckle rub in the hair. It was painful and degrading to be so treated, so war was declared in our hearts and minds. John Jay was too big to be attacked directly, so we tried to think of other ways of revenge. We discussed pushing him off the end of the dock, but if he was a good swimmer that would not be bad enough, and if he drowned we might go to jail. We would not mourn him, but he was not worth a jail sentence. We endured separately another scalp massage, and still had no good ideas for getting even. Opportunity would knock and good fortune would soon smile upon us.

John Jay did not seem to swim or explore or fish; he just hung around Cap'n Bill's. Bernard and I noticed he was interested in girls, particularly in three young ladies a year or two older than he who stayed in a cottage back from the beach. They came occasionally to the pavilion, sometimes spoke, but mostly acted remote and self-sufficient. They were pretty, though, and John Jay evidently thought so, too.

On the great day that came at last, I had led Bernard down to the Doxsee house, and we were hiking back to Cap'n Bill's. We sighted the three girls coming toward us followed by John Jay hopefully tagging along behind. They were about a hundred yards away. The beach was wide on this stretch except for a sort of peninsula of yucca and myrtle bushes that grew almost to the water's edge. It was about halfway between us and the three girls. On our side of the bushes was one of the goose gangs busily scratching and pecking at tender shoots and things. The great plan evolved suddenly, so I whispered to Bernard, who understood at once and nodded assent.

We gathered throwing clods and carefully approached the goose gang and the bushes. We were not visible to John Jay, but the girls had come back into view at the edge of the water. The geese were restive at our proximity, but not yet warlike. In a minute or two that seemed like an hour, the girls passed us with a nod, and John Jay hove into view. We leaped out in plain sight and yelled our war cry, "Hey, hey, old fat Blue Jay!" Then we flung our clay and turf clobber balls. Bernard fired at John Jay and I pelted the goose gang. We wheeled around and raced past the enraged geese and inland into the bushes. John Jay was enraged, too. He charged after us, around the point of brush, and right into the geese.

The ambush plan worked to perfection, even exceeding the hopes of the perpetrators. The geese went for John Jay. He tried to put on brakes and, oh happy day, slipped down in the plentiful goose droppings. Under a fury of flapping wings and hissing beaks he had trouble getting up. He skidded down again, but finally got to his feet and ran away from those furious geese. His white shirt and new white duck pants were coated black and green. They had smeared him hip and thigh. He ran away from the geese, away from the girls, straight for the Sound where he flopped down in the water and wallowed off the goose turd. Red-faced and blubbering, he arose from the sea and trudged back to the Inn. The girls shrieked with laughter while from our our hiding place we clapped our hands to our mouths to muffle our howls. The geese resumed feeding. We stayed away from John Jay until he went home. I decided that geese could be useful allies, if not close friends. Those geese were not so bad after all.

Then there were the island goats, not so many as the geese, but formidable. I knew two of them and did not want to know any more.

I had met Mr. Ballance's goat on the rare occasions when I had been pressed into service to carry buckets of sweet water to the cottage. This goat was a guard goat. He stood in his yard, lowered his head, and threatened intruders by baaaing goat profanity. He did not charge if the visitors kept a respectful distance.

The other goat was an attack goat. He lived across the salt marsh behind Aunt Ella's cottage and might have belonged to Mr. Maultby Bragg. Brother Sammy's friend Buddy Morgan, had been attacked. Buddy Morgan, who was not much bigger than the goat, had grabbed hold of his horns as the goat pushed him backwards down the path. "Please, Mr. Billy Goat, don't butt me!" he yelled until Mr. Bragg rescued him.

The attack goat liked to take his post near the end of a little one-plank wide foot bridge across the narrow outlet of the salt marsh. The goat had once chased Aunt Annie's children, Bill and Weegie, back across the bridge, and they were scared to use this short-cut to the stores 'round the Creek. Aunt Annie could not accept this behavior from a goat who acted like a troll. Rolling up her sleeves and jamming her sun hat firmly on her head, Aunt Annie led her shrinking children back across the bridge. The goat met them half way. Aunt Annie seized the goat by the horns and threw him off the bridge. They crossed in safety. I looked upon Aunt Annie with awe after learning all this. The goat was not much chastened for he continued to guard his bridge, but he did not mess around with Aunt Annie any more.

Far out-numbering other creatures inhabiting the beaches of the Sound shore were the mud fiddlers. They lived in holes in the black turf and in the edges of the marsh and scavenged food all along the water's edge in swarms. They seemed to signal each other somehow, for the swarms could change direction as a unit, or reverse course and go home to their holes. The crabs could pinch with their one large claw, but did not hurt much. Their shells bore a splotch of color that Sister said was a sunset, but it looked like just a blob to me. I wondered why the critters were called *fiddlers*. They certainly were not musical.

When Uncle Joe Bell compared a swarm of mud fiddlers to a Roman Legion, remarking that when they all raised their large claws in unison they were saluting "Hail, Caesar!" a plan naturally followed: to build a coliseum in the sand and use mud fiddlers as gladiators.

Lee and I constructed an oval arena of damp sand, with

upward slanting rows of seats and even an Emperor's box in the center of one side. The tide wrack furnished two tin cans for specimen legionnaires, each canful from a different swarm of mud fiddlers so they would not be friends. The two bloodthirsty spectators poured in the gladiators and anticipated the battle. The fiddlers, disinclined to fight as programmed, skittered up the bleachers, over the Emperor's box, and outside to freedom. We were not discouraged, and rebuilt the coliseum with straight-up walls using bottles and washed-ashore shingles. While we worked, Lee had the idea of using a large sand fiddler for a lion and the mud fiddlers as Christians.

Sand fiddlers were larger, aristocratic cousins of mud fiddlers; they lived in a cleaner looking hole in the sand and were sand colored. Their claws could draw blood. They were very fast running back to their dens, and hard to catch. Though they lived in sand, not mud, their homes were still holes. We hunted that night by moonlight, and finally caught a sand fiddler in a gallon can, where we kept him until morning. After breakfast we marched happily off to the games, picking up the can of lion on the way. The sand fiddler rattled around angrily. "Good," we thought, "he's mad." We poured the lion into the arena, observed that he could not scale the shingle walls, and ran off to capture a canful of mud fiddlers. With anticipation of carnage, we returned to dump the Christians in. The sand fiddler was gone—we forgot his digging ability! We gave up our plan in disgust. There was little companionship or entertainment in mud fiddlers.

Far more fauna lived in the waters surrounding the island than on it. We fished off the piers daily, catching pinfish and croakers, some of eating size, but most throw-backs. There were all sorts of interesting little creatures living in the crevices of the rock jetties, stuck to the piling of the piers, or buried beneath the sandbars. We liked to meet returning fishing parties to see all the kinds of fish they brought in.

The biggest creature we ever found was a nearly dead sting ray, triangular in shape, and big enough to cover the top of the wood cook stove. He was expiring from some injury when we found him, and our prodding with gigs and sharp sticks finished him off. He was tan on top, white on the bottom, and had a long, sharp tail like a sword blade. We had been told that his tail was deadly poison, so we were careful not to step on it. The ray had two oblong things, one on either side of his tail, that we thought looked like blackjacks. Billy immediately identified the critter as a rare burglar ray who always carried around his blackjacks.

I did not come across another burglar ray until the summer we met Wheeler, a year or two later. Wheeler was a little kid, younger than Lee or me, who followed us around just as we followed Sister and the girls and their boy friends. He was staying at the Nunnelee cottage with his mother and another house party. We tried to scare Wheeler away so he would not follow us. We did not want to hurt him, so we told him stories about sea noddies.

These fearful creatures were the invention of the father of an island friend of Brother Sammy. The sea noddies laid in wait underwater for solitary swimmers they could gobble up, a story supposed to deter young folk from swimming alone. Lee and I did not believe the tale any more than the older boys did, but it could be a useful story.

We told little Wheeler all about sea noddies. His hair stood on end; he was terrified; he loved the story. He kept asking more questions about sea noddies and we kept inventing more facts about their appeerence, their fangs and claws, and their hiding places. Wheeler shivered in delighted terror, stopped going swimming, and begged for more stories.

A few days later, as I was passing the Nunnelee cottage, I was recognized and summoned by Wheeler's mother. I had noticed her before and thought she was attractive, with sort of a picture show look. She had tightly waved hair, wore sleeveless sun dresses, and sported a long, black cigarette holder. She was not attractive that day, however. She stood on her porch, pointed that cigarette holder at me like a whip, and demanded that I leave Wheeler alone.

"Stop picking on him," she ordered. "You scared him to death with those sea monster lies you told him. You leave my boy alone and you stay away from here!"

I hurried off, seething with outraged innocence (a novel feeling). We had not picked on Wheeler nor hurt him. We told him scary stories, but Wheeler loved them and asked for more. I wished a real sea noddy would eat Wheeler's old mama.

A few days later, with Wheeler back hoping for more terror stories, we found the second burglar ray. This one was about the size of a towel and very ripe, for he had been dead a long time. I called Wheeler, assured him the water was too shallow for sea noddies, and showed him the dead ray. I explained to Wheeler that this was a rare and valuable find. The hide of burglar rays was the best and toughest kind of leather, I told Wheeler, if it was properly dried and cured. I said we could make belts and pistol holsters out of the ray, but first it had to be slowly dried out in a secret, shady place. I said I could not take it home to cure it because too many people would see it and want a share. Wheeler might want to take it to his cottage, which was close to the water, and hide it under the porch. I found an old coat hanger and made a long hook so Wheeler could tow the ray home. When I punched the wire hook through the creature's tough skin, the spurt of odor gave a fair sampling of what the porch would smell like later. After cautioning Wheeler not to step on the tail and to keep the plan secret, we watched him gingerly dragging the treasure. He reached the Nunnelee cottage and crawled underneath.

I obeyed Wheeler's mother and stayed away, but she was often in my thoughts. I savored the thought of her, cigarette holder and all, gasping in the miasma of old burglar ray.

The island abounded with other strange sea creatures besides sea noddies. We thought the strangest looking of the marine critters were the king crabs—some people called them horseshoe crabs. They had shells that looked like flat army helmets. They could be grabbed by their non-poisonous tails and lifted out of water, exposing their engine room and propulsion machinery underneath. They had two small claws up front and what looked like dozens of wriggling legs. They surely were ugly. Lee said their long, boney, triangular tails looked like Civil War bayonets. That intriguing picture impelled us to try to wrench loose the tails of a couple of big ones to carry in our belts. The king crabs were reluctant to give up their tails, so we threw them back overboard, convinced that dislocated tails would soon get well.

With swords still in mind, we managed to hack off two of the stiff leaves fron one of the giant yucca plants. We began to duel with the yucca swords until Mama stopped us. The leaves were needle sharp and dangerous weapons. The plant's local name, "Spanish Bayonet," is apt. Yucca grows prolifically in the sandy soil; some of the plants tower over ten feet tall. The long stalks of cream colored, bell-shaped flowers on top attracted the attention of even flower-unconscious boys. With all those swords and bayonets below, the flowers were unpickable.

Other wild flowers on the island were showy—as were the cultivated ones in yards and gardens—though we would have paid them little attention but for Aunt Lizzie's comments.

Lizzie was an avid gardener at home and carried her horticultural knowledge and curiousity to Ocracoke. She escorted us one day to the lighthouse to look at a lemon tree—or was it an orange tree?—growing there, a tropical tree that had no business at Ocracoke. On the way she pointed out several bushes with large, gaudy, red and yellow flowers called "Poincianas" or "Birds of Paradise," which were tropical, too. She showed us oleanders in several of the yards we passed, and big clumps of red and yellow cannas. We thought she called them candles. I had already heard of yaupon bushes when Lizzie pointed to a bunch of them growing with the myrtle and yucca. I had been told that the Indians and the settlers made tea from yaupon leaves and I wanted to try some. Aunt Lizzie said the leaves had to be harvested at the right time and dried and cured. She also said it was very healthful. I lost interest right then. It seemed too much trouble, but mainly, I figured, if it was good for you, it would not taste good.

Red-yellow-orange daisies grew all over the place in hardy clumps anywhere they could find space in the sun. On the island they were "Joe Bell Flowers," for nobody but Lizzie called them their proper name: gaillardias. Uncle Joe got credit for planting them. He had brought a packet of seeds when he first moved to Ocracoke and planted them in the yard at Bup's cottage. Their seeds are windborne, so they spread up and down the island, across the beaches and inlets, even to Hatteras and Portsmouth. They were the most widespread flowers on the island—and, I thought , the prettiest.

UNCLE JOE BELL

UNCLE JOE BELL WAS MY MOTHER'S UNCLE. He was above medium height, lean and rangy until his later years, when he encouraged a round, pot belly that looked like it belonged to somebody else. From under shaggy eyebrows, his bright blue eyes looked at the world with amusement.

I saw Uncle Joe at Ocracoke only that one time when he commented on mud fiddlers and Roman Legions, for he died soon thereafter. I remember him better when he crossed the Sound to visit us at home. He stayed at his brother's house, but he visited all his relatives, usually appearing at mealtime. Uncle Joe would politely decline an invitation to breakfast, dinner, or supper, and ask for just a cup of coffee. With only a little more persuasion he would eat a full meal, even though he had visited other tables just previously. A family expression developed from Uncle Joe's habits, so that anyone wanting something to eat would state, "I'll just take a cup of cahfee."

Uncle Joe dressed formally on his mainland visits in a dark suit and a necktie with a pearl stickpin in it. He was an interesting though pedantic speaker and told stories about Alaska and Eskimos, glaciers, seals and caribou steaks, an earthquake he experienced, and soldiers blowing up buildings. I loved to listen to him. Later, at family gatherings I heard Uncle Joe stories from various relatives, including some things strange to me, like "shotgun wedding." I too, began to cobble together a biography of Uncle Joe on hearsay, which took me years to assemble.

Joseph Nash Bell was born into a many-branched family that was spread through the eastern counties of the state. His branch lived in Washington and were jewelers by trade. Uncle Joe left home in 1864 to join the Confederate army—at age fourteen. His military career was blighted when a family friend sent him back home by a cavalry patrol.

He entered the University when he was eighteen but dropped out after one year. He next took a course at a business college, which he completed even though he did not like it. A family conference decided he should attend watchmakers school to learn more about the family business. He liked the course and learned engraving and other facets of the jeweler's trade. He also enjoyed the social life with pretty girls in that far-off Yankee city.

Upon his return home, Uncle Joe joined his father and brothers in the family's store. Washington has always had an ample supply of pretty girls and Uncle Joe knew them all. One young lady succeeded in taking him to church with her, but when her mother insisted he come to Sunday dinner, Uncle Joe got skittish. He packed his bags, told the young lady he was off to seek his fortune, and boarded the next steamer to Norfolk.

That was why Uncle Whitey had talked about avoiding a shotgun wedding. Uncle Whitey laughed about it, but Mama flared at him, "That's not true. She was a nice girl. It never got that far!" Whatever the reason, several months later his mother received a post card from Uncle Joe saying he was in the Klondike mining gold.

He did not mine long. Uncle Joe found that gold mining was dirty, dangerous work and that mining camps were harsh, dreary places to live. He sold his claim, and moved to Dawson, the metropolis of the miners, where he rented a store. He renewed his contacts in the jewelry trade, unpacked his tools, and started work as Dawson's premier watchmaker. Far more gold flowed into his hands than he could ever have dug up himself. When the goldrush began to decline in the Klondike, Uncle Joe moved to a new gold-field in Alaska and continued to extract gold from miners. When satisfied that he had enough money, Uncle Joe took ship for California to enjoy himself.

He made several sea voyages. Whether he shipped as sailor, ship's officer, or chronometer keeper is not known. He was in San Francisco during the great earthquake and resulting fire. He decided California was not such a safe place to live, came back east and worked in New York for several years.

In his middle years, the Southland called, so Uncle Joe came home again. He did not enter the family business, nor try to renew old contacts. Instead he bought a buggy, a horse named Mabel, and a stock of watches and jewelry. He traveled the eastern counties, a wandering jeweler and itinerant watchmaker. When Mabel died, Uncle Joe decided he needed yet another change.

When Grandpa, his brother-in-law, bought his second Ocracoke cottage, Uncle Joe recognized his opportunity. His proposal to Grandpa was mutually beneficial. Uncle Joe got free housing, the solitude he craved at times, and neighbors who were friendly and helpful, but not intrusive. Grandpa got a year-round care-taker and maintenance man. In the summer when the cottages were full, Uncle Joe moved into one of the porch rooms. While the island was infested with summer people, he got all the social life he sometimes enjoyed.

One visitor he enjoyed seeing was the author Rex Beach. He had visited and written about the same north country where Uncle Joe had been. Mr. Beach visited Ocracoke on his yacht which had a cabin as long as a railroad car. Young Harry O'Neal of Ocracoke remembered rowing Uncle Joe out to the yacht where the two men spent the evening yarning, boasting, and drinking. Uncle Joe did like a toddy at times.

Strong drink was hard to get on the island, and Uncle Joe usually tippled on his visits to the mainland. One time, however, at Ocracoke, he was celebrating some memorable event known only to him when he overestimated his capacity and, while trying to dip out a cup of chaser, he fell headfirst in the cistern. The cottage was full of family, and two of his nieces rushed to his rescue and extracted him. The old man choked, gurgled, and spluttered. As dignified as circumstances permitted, he addressed his salvors, "I thank you young ladies, though I musht remind you that I am perfectly capable of taking care of myshelf."

Uncle Joe repaired watches and clocks for islanders and visitors, and made rings and small jewelry. He worked as much as he wanted to, but no more. He was elected and served as magistrate of Ocracoke, learnimg to perform the marriage ceremony he had avoided for himself. He was a happy man.

His lasting souvenir of his days in California are the gaillardias he planted. His other horticultural effort did not long survive him. He planted a double row of garlic which he needed for his exotic cookery, for Uncle Joe had collected foreign recipes during his travels. He cooked a sea turtle one of the island fishermen had given him while Mama's brother Harry was staying with him. When Uncle Harry peered in the pot and saw all the turtle's parts that were included in the stew, he fled the cottage to take his meals elsewhere. "A great delicacy among the Alaskan Indians," Uncle Joe boasted afterward.

Uncle Joe's usual dress on the island was less formal and more distinctive than his mainland clothes. He wore a long-sleeved white shirt without a collar or tie but with a gold collar-button closing the neck. In the collar button he had mounted a little garnet, a twinkling trademark. He wore khaki trousers held up by wide red suspenders. The waistband of his trousers enclosed his round belly like the cone holds the scoop of ice cream. On cool mornings he put on a black alpaca coat. He looked comfortable, if unique.

Uncle Joe's final departure was as abrupt as his first. He strolled out of his room one fine summer morning, suffered a stroke, and fell off the porch. He was dead when he hit the ground. The yard where he fell was sprinkled with Joe Bell flowers.

Sister Mary saw him fall and screamed for Aunt Lizzie, who took charge. She asked some of the island men to lay him out, asked Mr. Austin at the lighthouse to send the emergency wire to his brothers, and sent word to our family by the boat next morning. Ocracoke neighbors built his coffin and conducted the funeral as soon as his brothers arrived. They buried him in a corner of the lot at Bup's second cottage. Uncle Joe's enduring memorial, clumps of Joe Bell flowers, grow by his grave.

ISLANDERS

WE MET MORE ISLAND PEOPLE when we stayed with Aunt Lizzie than during the more convivial month with Mama. Aunt Lizzie's old-timey manners probably pleased the Ocracokers more than the house-party atmosphere at Bup's cottage. Too, Lizzie had been coming to the island for more summers than anybody else in the family, and she knew all the adult Ocracokers. But islanders of the younger generation were attracted to the house party.

The Braggs—Mr. Bragg, who was often called Cap'n Gary because he owned a fishing boat, and his wife, Miss Lena—were the closest neighbors to Bup's cottage as well as friends of Aunt Lizzie. Mr. Bragg, large and leathery looking, was always busy with fishing parties, work on his house or his boat, and other incomprehensible grown-up business. He was friendly, but mostly aloof to us.

Miss Lena stayed even busier than Mr. Bragg, but she sometimes stopped to talk to us when we came in with Doss. She planned meals, cooked and supervised a succession of island girls who helped run the big boarding house. Somebody at the cottage said Miss Lena ran a training school for house maids. I thought she was pretty if worn-looking, even if she was an old lady. I considered any female over thirty an old lady.

Another fixture of the Bragg's entourage was Julius Bryant, a member of the island's only black family. He was a few years older than me and acted very adult and business-like. He was Mr. Bragg's assistant, executive officer, and mate on the boat. Julius had a formidable pocket knife that he used to gut and scale fish, cut loose sting rays, or cut bait. He could handle a boat, rake clams, or repair nets. We admired Julius and all his skills. He, in turn, liked to show off for young visiting boys, wearing his wide grin that displayed an array of big white teeth. He was the only one who would take time to remove the ugly toadfish we sometimes caught. Otherwise we had to cut the line and lose the hook, for toadfish reportedly could and would bite off a finger.

Mr. Bragg was the cause of Lizzie's getting angry with me the time we all went 'round the Creek. No, not the cause, I quickly modify the thought, but the reason. What I said caused it. Lizzie hardly ever got angry with me, and when she did, I sure did not like it. She looked different—the way I imagined God or George Washington would look if angry. She talked different, too.

It happened the summer Aunt Lizzie, Lee, and I stayed in Bup's cottage. Mr. Bragg's gas boat was tied up at the end of his pier after he and Julius had landed a fishing party. Julius had gone home when Mr. Bragg stopped by the cottage and asked Lizzie if we would like to ride in the boat when he moved her around to his dock in the Creek. He knew how much we liked boats. He would go right after supper, he said. Lizzie agreed with thanks.

An hour later Mr. Bragg beckoned to us, so we followed him out on the pier and boarded the gas boat. It was a short but pleasant trip along the shore. Mr. Bragg even burned a little extra gas to circle out in the Sound and give us a good view of the island. The flicker of oil lamps began to appear in windows. Mr. Bragg piloted his boat into the Creek and moored to his dock. We all climbed ashore and started home along the sandy path.

That was when I said it. Maybe a venomous mosquito bit me then, or maybe it was a devil. Without thinking, but plainly speaking, I grumbled, "I wouldn't have come if I hadda known I had to walk back."

Mr. Bragg just wheeled around and stared for a second, but Aunt Lizzie was aghast. She reared up and shook me by the shoulder.

"Why you ungrateful wretch!" she flared. "How dare you speak to Mr. Bragg like that?"

I realized I had made a bad mistake. I said I did not mean it and tried to laugh. When we parted from Mr. Bragg in the road by the cottage, I was fervent in my thanks for the boat ride. Mr. Bragg did not hold a grudge, for later in the month he invited us to ride around the Creek again. This time I kept my mouth shut, except to say I had a good time.

Aunt Lizzie had the unique ability to dominate people by will power alone while showing her hot temper. She used it rarely, only when she thought someone had behaved improperly or disrespectfully. I once heard my mother and father discussing this characteristic of Aunt Lizzie. Mama said, "Lizzie talks like a character in a Victorian novel when she's angry. In fact, she *is* a Victorian." Daddy said she talked like his Aunt Venetia." Mama said, "Well she was a Victorian, too."

I didn't know if Aunt Lizzie was Victorian or Venetian, but I did know better than to upset her that way again. I did not like being petrified.

The next summer I made another voyage with Mr. Bragg. This one was in a flatbed truck and we rode way down the beach to Mr. Bragg's camp. I did not even know Mr. Bragg had a truck or a camp until I was invited to help pick up some things at the camp. Mr. Bragg said we would leave in an hour when the tide was right. As I ran over to tell Mama where I was going, I puzzled over what the tide had to do with a trip in a truck. Maybe we were going to ford a creek. I climbed in the cab with Mr. Bragg, but did not want to ask about the tide. Maybe I would learn it by watching.

We wound through the middle of the island, across the deep sand of the beach, straight to the ocean. Mr. Bragg turned the truck left at the edge of the water, where the outgoing tide had left a ribbon of damp, firmly packed sand. It was as good as a racetrack and we seemed to fly along, only slowing and swerving to avoid wreck timbers. It was almost as exciting as sailing, speeding straight along with the breakers surging almost up to the wheels. Even grown-ups would like this. Mr. Bragg appeared to enjoy it, for he sat hunched over the steering wheel, grinning and glancing sideways at me and the breakers.

At some landmark invisible to me, but known to Mr. Bragg, we turned left again and groaned over a sandy track inland. Mr. Bragg turned the truck around and switched off the engine. I asked if we were at Down Below. Mr. Bragg shook his head and said, "Great Swash. Come along." (He never did talk much.)

We walked inland, around a sand dune, and came to a small gray shack in the bushes. A few cedar trees grew near it and a big live oak hovered over it. A path led further away from the ocean and toward the Sound, now visible and sparkling in the sun. Mr. Bragg told me I could look around, but not to go far, because we would not stay long.

I trotted along the path to the Sound shore and out on a short pier. The shore was sandy right at the pier, but marshy on both sides. I discovered another silvery-gray board building, a low open front shed. Going inside, I found a lot of wood decoys segregated into piles—goose, brant, and duck. I thought this would be a good camp site for the exploring expedition Lee and Billy and I had talked about. I decided to ask Mr. Bragg if there was a water pump at the camp.

Mr. Bragg hailed me a few minutes later, so I ran back to the shack. He picked up a bundle of net and motioned toward two lumpy tow sacks. I hefted a sack, which was full but not really heavy; it contained a few coils of rope but mostly cork net floats. After placing these on the truck, we both came back for another load. Mr. Bragg lashed the bundles and bags in place and we mounted the cab. We drove through the deep sand again and turned right onto the ocean speedway. The ride back was so much fun that I forgot to ask about a water pump at the camp.

But I did not forget to thank Mr. Bragg for the ride, and to promise to help him haul stuff anytime. I made myself a promise, too: "I got to find out how to find out about tides. Daddy or Bup'll know."

Aunt Lizzie liked to walk 'round the Creek in the afternoon to visit the post office, the stores, or friends in their homes. One of the stores near the post office was Big Ike O'Neal's. He was the biggest man on the island and the lightest-footed of the square dancers. I thought his daughter Elizabeth was the prettiest of the island girls, though there were many others. (From my association with the house-party girls, I was developing a high standard of feminine beauty.) When sent to get something from a store, my buddies and I usually chose Mr. Big Ike's store because of his jovial greeting. He sometimes told us sea stories from his experiences in schooners.

One day Aunt Lizzie and I visited Mr. Big Ike at his house on one of the winding sandy roads behind the stores. In the front yard I admired a big bush full of the largest figs I had ever seen. Mr. Big Ike gave me a paper bag and insisted that I pick some figs. I picked gladly. Aunt Lizzie said they were called pound figs, although Elizabeth said they were extra large red figs. Whatever they were, they were good eating.

There was another Mr. Ike O'Neal on the island and Lizzie knew him, too. He was called Red Ike to distinguish him from

Big Ike. He was captain of the Washington boat, so I thought of him as Captain Ike. He did not seem quite so austere off the ship as on. Lizzie also introduced me to Captain Ike's wife and to his twin brother Walter.

Frequently we boys walked 'round the Creek when *Russell L.* or *Preston* was in port. We hung around the dock watching cargo being unloaded, getting in the way, and sometimes, happily, being invited to come aboard. On one such visit, while I was sitting on the hatch cover listening to Cap'n Red Ike talk to a friend, I heard about pound figs again. I should have recognized a "tall tale," for both Pa and Uncle Ed liked that form of humor. Anyhow, Cap'n Ike told his friend about the time he was becalmed at sea for a week. Their food gave out, he said, and he and his crew lived on two pound figs and a case of condensed milk. That was why he did not eat figs any more. I began to fit out a sea story from Cap'n Ike's tale. I imagined Captain Ike confronting a half mutinous crew, as he carved equal slices from a pound fig as big as a watermelon. And with a cutlass. Captain Bligh could not have done it better.

The mail boat came from Atlantic, N.C. at five o'clock in the afternoon. She stopped first at Cap'n Bill's and sometimes at Mr. Bragg's pier before docking in the Creek and delivering the mail bags to Mr. Howard, the postmaster. He would lug them into the post office and lock the doors while he put up the mail. Sometimes his wife helped him with a big mail. I never met Mrs. Howard. In fact, I stayed out of her way on account of the story I had heard about her hot temper.

One lady I knew rode to the post office on one of the beach trucks. She was wearing her bathing suit and sat on the truck while others of her party went in for the mail. Although the lady was wrapped in a big beach towel over her bathing suit, Mrs. Howard thought she was dressed improperly, and threatened to pour boiling water on her if she tried to come in.

When the mail was at last sorted, Mr. Howard unlocked the doors and the islanders would stream in to take their mail from their boxes. The summer people had to ask for theirs at the window. Occasionally Mr. Howard stepped out on the porch to call names and hand out the mail. I never got much mail, but I still liked to go to the post office.

When Aunt Lizzie carried me to the post office on my first visit, she had introduced me to Mr. Howard. Sister told me that Mr. Big Ike's daughter Elizabeth was engaged to Mr. Howard's son Wahab. She said the couple attended the square dances together and consulted about which dance partner each one could have. I was in love with Elizabeth O'Neal, but decided to keep it a secret in case Wahab did not like it.

The trip to the post office was fun. Often the entire house party attended the mail call, for it was a social event for both visitors and islanders. To me and my buddies it ranked just behind meeting the Washington boat and just ahead of the square dances. Everybody enjoyed milling around the yard, laughing and talking. If the mail sorting took a long time, we licked on ice cream cones from Walter O'Neal's ice cream parlor. If the sorting took an extra long time, the girls said Mr. Howard was reading the post cards.

VISITORS

KIN FOLK CAME IN CONTINUAL STREAMS to stay a night, a week, or a month at the cottage. Other visitors to the island came by to see us during their stay. All were welcomed.

Mr. Mayer was the first visitor who impressed me. He stayed in Mr. Bragg's guest cottage right behind Bup's house. Mr. Mayer was a tall, husky man with a shiny bald head. He was bigger than Mr. Bragg. He was the most visible of the Braggs' guests because he liked to walk around in the evenings. He fished with Mr. Bragg nearly every day. They went off early in the boat and came back late in the afternoon with, usually, lots of fish. Mr. Mayer supplied the Braggs with fish and often brought fish over to Mama's house party: puppy drum for frying, great big drum in roasting size, or sometimes sheepshead, good-eating, ugly fish with teeth like people. I learned he was a Yankee and a big city man, but I had met other Yankees who were acceptable people. Mr. Mayer was unlike the other Yankees I knew, as though, maybe, he was a kind of foreign prince, captured, civilized, and sent to Ocracoke to fish. He came to the island so many summers that he became a fixture, almost like Mr. Bragg or Julius.

Several boys and girls, Bragg grandchildren, were around

for me to join in games and expeditions. When choosing sides or selecting an "it," I had learned the old rhyme: *Eenie, meenie, miney, moe,* which involved catching a Nigger, or sometimes a toadfrog, by the toe and then letting him go. The new acquaintances had a new, harsher sounding chant that went:

Akka, bakka, soda cracker, Akka, bakka boo—
If your father chews tobacca, He's a dirty Jew.

I went along with the rhyme, but I did not really like it. Daddy did not chew tobacco, but Uncle George did and he certainly was not dirty. Miss Lena Bragg put a stop to the use of the new rhyme. Doss announced that "Grandmama says we can't say that any more because Mr. Mayer is a Jew and he wouldn't like it."

I looked at Mr. Mayer with new curiosity. I wanted more information. I had heard the word Jew before, but did not really know what it meant. That night at supper I asked , "What's a Jew?" After a brief pause, Mama asked why I wanted to know. I explained about the forbidden rhyme. She approved of its non-use, then said, "A Jew is somebody who goes to a different kind of church."

"Oh," I answered, "Like Aunt Tootie?" When Uncle Harry married Aunt Tootie, I had heard somebody say she was a Catholic, and asked, "What's a Catholic?" I got the same answer about going to a different church. "No," Mama answered, "Jews and Catholics are not the same."

That answer was not good enough. I mused on the subject. Mr. Mayer, big and tough-looking, was nothing like Aunt Tootie, who was small and pretty. They indeed looked like they went to different "different churches." I knew there was a Catholic church in Washington that seemed similar to most of the other churches, except it was small and had some statues in the front yard. There was no church for Jews that I knew about. There were lots of different churches in town: Episcopal, Presbyterian, Methodists, Disciples, Baptists, Holy Rollers, and others unremembered. I could ask Aunt Lizzie about different churches when we went home, although I had once heard Lizzie remark that there were Presbyterians and others.

I started to think about what I had heard about Jews. First, there were a lot of Jews in the Sunday School lessons. I liked the stories about Joshua and David and Goliath, but could not identify Mr. Mayer with any of them. The Ben Hur book was not much use to me because I could not remember which ones were Jews, Romans, or Christians. A sort of answer came from a story Lizzie had read about King Richard the Lion-Hearted. He was fighting King Saladin, a Saracen, in Jerusalem, where the Jews came from. The Saracens were tough soldiers, though not as good as King Richard's men. Mr. Mayer might be kin to them.

I soon learned that the Saracen, after fishing, liked talking. He would often stroll over to the cottage to sit on the porch during the interval between supper and our departure for the square dance at Cap'n Bill's. He liked and listen to the girl's chatter, but he did not accompany us to the pavilion; he went home instead.

Mr. Mayer sometimes told the young folks stories of his sea voyages and fishing trips in other places. He seemed to enjoy the children's company as well as the grown-ups. I thought Mr. Mayer had only one fault—he did not have his own yacht. Otherwise he was an admirable friend.

Mr. Mayer had a talent often called upon by the younger set. He was adept at first aid, possibly a heritage from his ancestors' wars with King Richard. Before the invention of band-aids, the Saracen's ability to quickly patch cuts with a square of gauze and a strip of adhesive tape was much appreciated. We relied on Mr. Mayer even though he used iodine instead of mercurochrome or witch hazel, neither of which burned.

I got two more pieces of information about Mr. Mayer second hand from the old people's conversations. Mr. Mayer's wife was dead and he was supposed to have a lot of money. These pieces of information, it seemed, were of considerable interest to a lady from Washington who was visiting the island. (Uncle Whiting,

Mama's other brother, said the lady was a walking advertisement for the island, because the sea and sun had turned her hair bright yellow.)

This active widow lady had met Mr. Mayer while visiting the Braggs and at Bup's cottage. She had met him at the Post Office and on Mr. Bragg's pier. After meeting Mr. Mayer she sent a rush order to her sister at home for a pair of lavender beach pajamas.

The next morning, she just happened to be on the pier when Mr. Bragg, Julius, and Mr. Mayer were loading the boat. She told Mr. Mayer how much she had always loved fishing, so he invited her to go with them on a fishing trip for sheepshead near a wreck over towards Portsmouth. (Uncle Whitey saw her get in the boat on the appointed day, "all gleaming in purple and gold," he said.) When they returned in mid-afternoon, Mr. Mayer escorted the lady back to the Pamlico Inn. He stopped by the cottage before he went home and reported that they had not had much luck fishing. Then he went home for supper.

One of the interested observers of the campaign asked Mr. Bragg if anything was developing between the lady and Mr. Mayer. Mr. Bragg just grinned and shook his head. There was to be no wedding of different churches. It was later the next summer before Julius released a little more information. "We hadn't hardly come abreast of the inlet," he said, "when she throwed up in his lap."

Another visitor who came to the cottage was a friend of Aunt Margaret and Uncle Thomas Hill. He came alone, a stray from a fishing party who were all staying at the Pamlico Inn. Monte did not fish, so he visited during the afternoon and rejoined his friends in the evening. Aunt Margaret said that Monte had held a big job up north, but now he was just relaxing. Uncle Thomas Hill remarked that he always seemed to be relaxed when there was work to do. When Margaret and Thomas Hill left at the end of the week, Monte still spent afternoons at Bup's cottage.

I thought Monte was worth close examination for he was a sharp dresser. He wore the first pair of loafers I had ever seen, even though I did not know what to call them. With his open-collared shirt Monte wore a sort of silk, backwards neckerchief tied in a loose bow knot, of a sort I had seen only in the picture shows.

Monte spent a lot of time talking to Sister and the girls and to old ladies, but he spent most of his afternoons dozing in a canvas beach chair. Sometimes, when nobody was around except my spying eye, Monte pulled out a neat little curved silvery bottle and gulped a quick gurgle. I kept up my silent watch.

If I was too noisy, Monte would grunt disapproval. One afternoon when the shipyard was very busy and Mama and the girls were gone, Monte peered grumpily around the corner and asked if we were through hammering yet. Another time he directed us to play somewhere else.

Monte's company quickly palled for us, but Mama and the girls seemed to enjoy his conversation. I was not happy to hear that Monte, separated from his party for a couple of days, would be using one of the porch rooms until they returned for him, although he continued to spend his evenings in the more convivial atmosphere of the Inn. I was glad to be rid of him even part of the time.

Old Monte fluffed himself out for the ladies, but did not bother to be affable to men and children. One male cousin told me that during the time Monte stayed at his house, he spent many hours trying to think of a way, any way, to get rid of Monte permantly and not be blamed for it. My buddies and I did not like him and neither did the Ocracokers because of his overbearing manner.

Late one evening, almost bedtime, one of the island young men called Lee and me out into the road. He was one of the Gaskills, I thought, or he may have been a Styron.

"I want to fix old Mounty," he said, "have ye got a hatchet?"

"You ain't going to kill him are you?" I was surprised, but not really disapproving. It was a way to get rid of Monte, and with somebody else doing it.

"No, no. I'm not gonna hurt 'im," he answered, "Mounty's drunk over to the pavilion. I just wanta cut some bushes to 'fix his biscuits.'"

I was interested, and said the shipyard did not have a hatchet but did have a saw and a pocket knife. "Ye go get 'em and ye can come with me," responded the young man.

Lee and I, with saw and knife, followed our new buddy along the path and across the Turtle Ditch. Here, just where the path jogged to the right before the bridge, the islander quickly sawed some of the myrtle bushes growing on the ditch bank. With the skill acquired in building duck blinds, he punched the bushes in the ground right across the path, masking the bridge. In the dark, it looked like the path continued straight—right into the ditch. He whispered "Come on," re-crossed the bridge and hurried on to the road. We followed.

We stood quietly until we heard somebody coming along the other end of the path, singing, or rather bellowing, a song.

"That's Mounty," the islander said as he handed back the saw. "Get out here in the mornin' and throw that bresh away. I'll be out to my nets at sunup."

Things happened fast. The singing cut off. We heard a great splash, then more splashing, then more bellowing, this time cussing. Some of the words were new to us. The Ocracoker departed with a last, "Don't forget the bresh." I wondered how Monte had made the Ocracoker so mad with him. With Monte it would not be hard to do.

We ran back to the cottage and sat quietly in the dark shipyard. The girls were all upstairs and most of the lamps were out but Mama was still up. She told us to come to bed. Before we could comply, up lurched Monte, dripping and bedraggled, considerably less tipsy and no longer cussing so much.

"Slipped off that damn bridge. I think I sprained my hip. That bridge is unsafe. It may be rotten. May I borrow a flashlight? I think I lost something." Monte fidgeted while Mama looked for the flashlight. She returned, trapped between laughter and sympathy, and anxious for Monte to leave.

"Can the boys help you look for something?" she offered.

"Yes," mumbled Monte, and started back to the bridge, his flashlight beam staggering on ahead. We followed joyfully but silently. He could not hear our grins and did not turn around as he told us, "I lost my silver flask."

We followed while Monte searched up and down the banks of the Turtle Ditch, around and under the bridge, and on the path. Monte did not even notice the stuck-in myrtle branches, and we made an effort to walk over them. The search was in vain, for no flask was visible in the black water at night. With a last volley of cussing, Monte gave up.

Mama was still on the porch. Monte groaned to her that his precious flask was gone. "Probably already stolen by some thieving native." Mama gave him one of her quick, hot answers to that. She let him know that she had never known an Ocracoker to steal anything. Monte retired to his room, still fuming. He was mad at somebody, but he did not know who.

I went out to the Turtle Ditch at first light. Most of the camouflage bushes were knocked over, so I finished disposing of them. The banks of the ditch looked like a herd of hippos had wallowed there, where Monty had floundered in and floundered out. I mused over the idea that the cut brush had not really been necessary, for in his condition Monte would have fallen in anyway. The Turtle Ditch caught a lot of people.

Just before leaving, I spotted Monty's little flask, just visible in the black water, lying in the mud with its cap unscrewed, secured by a little chain. I had a feeling that I ought to uphold the honor of the Ocracokers by not giving in to somebody like Monte. I knew, like Mama, that nobody would have stolen the thing. I thought they might have drunk the stuff in it, though. I could just reach it with one of the myrtle limbs. I pushed it down into the invisible depths.

I looked forward to telling Cousin Tommy how we got rid of Monte, even if it was not permanent.

The next weekend we were having a rare Sunday morning breakfast with no extra guests. We had not even met the Washington boat at Cap'n Bill's, as we were expecting neither relatives nor close friends, nor any freight. Lee and I were preoccupied with plans for a trip to the ocean beach that afternoon. A shout from the grass road out front got everyone's attention.

"Hello," the voice called, "will you let a wandering minstrel come in?"

It was a familiar sounding voice, but nobody identified it. Sister arose and went out on the front porch. "Why it's Zoph," she called back. Then to the man in the road, "Come on in, Zoph. You're a nice surprise. You're just in time for breakfast." She led him inside. All the girls stood up to welcome him; Mama seated him at the table and went to the kitchen to get tableware. Zoph was a favorite of them all.

"Don't go to any trouble, Miss Nita," he told Mama. "I had breakfast at the Inn. But I might take one of those biscuits and a slice of ham. I just wanted to walk over and say hello to y'all. I've got to go back and unpack and settle in." Then he ate some eggs, a piece of puppy drum, another biscuit, and some coffee.

Zoph Potts was an old friend of us all. He had been courting Billy's sister Lou Gillam, who was not with the present house party, but Zoph did not restrict himself to Lou Gillam alone: he liked all girls.

Zoph was a medium-sized young man, not really skinny, but sort of bony looking. He had a wide-mouthed smile and bright hazel eyes. He had a happy nature, a quick wit, and a friendly manner that made him popular with all ages. He was also a skilled pianist and that was why he had come to Ocracoke. As he enjoyed his second breakfast, Zoph told us Cap'n Bill had hired him to play the piano for the square dances. He told us there was an accordian player from Elizabeth City and a fiddler from Manteo, who was the leader, and himself in the band. Cap'n Bill's previous piano player, a man from Norfolk, had left the island in a hurry when his whisky gave out.

Zoph invited us to come to the pavilion that afternoon, if we were so inclined, when he would try out the piano. He liked to play requests for people. Cap'n Bill said he could play extra concerts anytime he wanted to. Zoph said he had one other job requirement besides playing for the dances. He was supposed to mingle with the guests at mealtime and to notify Miss Annie or Sue Dimock (Miss Annie's assitant and niece) if anything ran short at the tables. Dining room duties were no hardship, Zoph grinned, as he had been told that the food was very good at the Pamlico Inn and he loved seafood. He thanked Mama for the breakfast, waved goodby to the girls and strode off to the Inn to unpack and to take his dinner time post.

Zoph confided to Sister that he was getting room, board, and five dollars a week for playing six nights a week and for his other part-time social duties. I did not know anybody else who was housed, fed, and paid anything at all to come to Ocracoke. It sounded like a nice job.

Lee and I were not particularly interested in music but thought we might go to the pavilion if we got back from the beach in time. After he left, the girls agreed that Zoph would improve the dance band a whole lot. He could read music, they said, and play anything. He could play by ear, too, whatever that meant. I asked Sister later to explain the term to me, as I did not think my mental image could be correct—Zoph bent over the keyboard, pressing the keys with his ears.

Lee and I returned from the beach earlier than expected. The boy and girl who had invited us on the beach trip had a name that sounded like Zunkle or Jonkle. The children were dull and Mr. and Mrs. Junkle were mad about something and sat apart, hissing at each other. After about an hour, Mr. Junkle hailed a passing truck and brought us home.

Lee had stumped his toe on a board, so he thought he would lie back and read the rest of the afternoon. Both of us were reading *Treasure Island* and it was Lee's turn to have the book. Aunt Lizzie had read it aloud long ago but now we were studying it on our own. I had no other books I wanted to read, so I ambled over to see what was happening at Cap'n Bill's.

I heard the piano before I climbed over the stile. I trotted out on the dock, turned into the pavilion, and joined Sister, the whole crowd of house-party girls, and a bunch of other people. They were standing around the piano or sitting near it. Zoph was playing, glancing around, and smiling. Piano playing must be hard work, I thought, because Zoph was sweating on his forehead and on the little bald patch on top of his head.

Every one of the girls had a special song she wanted and Zoph played them all. After a while, one of the men in the bunch brought Zoph a cold co'cola, so he took a break. He swung around to face the crowd, grinned at them and said, "It's a pretty good old piano. Better than I expected in this sea air. Did I get to everybody's request?" He saw me standing next to Sister and asked, "How about you, Mac? What's your favorite song?"

I was flustered at being singled out but, remembering *Treasure Island*, I asked Zoph to play "Fifteen Men on a Dead Man's Chest." The crowd laughed at my request, but Zoph did not laugh, and answered seriously, "I've heard of that song, but I don't know the tune. If you'll sing it, I'll try to play it." I was in an agony of embarrassment—I did not know the tune and I was far too shy to sing in a crowd. I blushed between my freckles and stammered that I could not sing it. Zoph recognized my discomfort and quickly swiveled back to the piano. "How about this one then, if you like sea chanteys?" He played a rousing rendition of

"Anchors Aweigh." I recovered and decided that Zoph Potts was all right.

Cap'n Bill bustled through the dance hall as the concert ended. Zoph talked privately to him for a minute, then turned back to the girls and invited them to the dining room for ice cream. He included me. Sister answered that we would love to, but we would pay for our own ice cream as there were too many of us for Zoph to invite. He said he had already arranged it. I did not know who paid, but I went willingly to eat my block of red, white, and brown ice cream. It was the only time I ever ate anything in the Pamlico Inn dining room, for we had plenty of good food at the cottage and never dined out.

The custom of eating Neopolitan ice cream on Sunday afternoon had evolved on the island. Everybody, not just hotel guests, could take advantage of Cap'n Bill's special import service. The Saturday night boat always brought a heavy, smoking, wooden box for the Pamlico Inn. A truck from the Maola Ice Cream Company in Washington delivered it just before sailing time. The box travelled wrapped in quilts in the hold, and it was filled with blocks of ice cream packed in dry ice. Cap'n Bill stored the box in a cool place and sold all of it that was surplus to his hotel guest's needs. I gobbled it up (while thinking I really liked Mrs. Styron's condensed milk-fresh fruit kind better).

I returned to the cottage with musical research on my mind. Lee had laid *Treasure Island* aside for a while, so I could check on what I wanted. I knew that lots of times books had stuff printed in the back after the main story ended, but I found no musical section. I did learn, as I leafed through the pages, that the song meant a wooden sea chest, not fifteen men standing on top of a dead pirate.

Zoph visited all over our part of the island. I saw him rowing a boat with a young lady sister's age who had promised to marry me when I grew up. She was a Pantegonian named Miriam Shavender, a name I thought was so pretty I repeated it to myself often. She saw me glaring at her and flashed me a big smile, so I forgave Zoph his intrusion. Some years later, Miriam stopped by our house in Washington to tell me she was breaking our engagement so she could marry another Pantegonian. We enjoyed acting sad about it, but I was really relieved because I could not yet support her. Miriam's clothes looked expensive.

During one of his afternoon concerts, Zoph announced "something inspirational." He made the piano sound like breaking waves and watery tinkles, and mixed in songs about the sea. He had eaten nine clam fritters at dinner, while his neighbor at the table urged him to go for a dozen. He called his new tune "An Ode to Clam Fritters," but even Zoph could not make the piano sound like a clam.

He talked to everybody—fishermen, boat captains, and visitors. He liked to talk about cooking to Mama. He asked her about boiled drum. His friend at the table had showed him how to mix the white flakes of fish with chopped onions and hard boiled eggs on a bed of mashed potatoes, and to sprinkle on top fried bacon chips. Zoph thought it was wonderful. Mama agreed and explained how she baked a big drum in the oven with some of the same things.

Zoph stayed busy with his duties at the hotel and his assumed duties as social director, whether aboard Cap'n Bill's beach truck or at various cottages. He was always careful to return to the Inn on time. Most afternoons he played in the pavilion for a while and every night but Sunday he played dance music with the little band. The girls all agreed with Charlotte when she said that Cap'n Bill certainly got his money's worth when he hired Zoph.

But Zoph surprised all of us one afternoon when he came to the cottage to tell us goodbye, saying that he was going home on the Washington boat the next morning. To the shocked girls he seemed stunned, even though he was smiling and joking as usual.

"Mr. Gaskill fired me," he explained, "He said I ate too much.

He said my piano playing was fine and all the hotel guests liked to have me around, but he could not afford to feed me."

Zoph asked for some coffee and the girls raced to get it. The girls all babbled at once how terrible Cap'n Bill was while Zoph sipped his coffee. He stood up to leave, hesitated, and said, "I had a job lined up as bookkeeper at the Eureka Mill. I reckon I'll take it, but I sure do hate to leave the island." He flashed a big grin before his farewell, "I guess I might compose a funeral march for inn keepers on the way home."

A variety of other visitors came to the cottage. One young man from Chapel Hill knew Charlotte's brother. His special talent was imitating a steam piano, the thing they played at the circus. He called it a calliope, and his "poodle-eedle, poodle-eedle, poodle-eedle-poo" resounded up and down the beach. He was entertaining for a little while.

The car-proud boy who followed him was not. This one's guaranteed second sentence, after telling us his name was "I got a Packard." He did not bring the thing with him, and I was not much interested anyway. A boat would have been different.

There were even more visitors to the island in the later summers. The Braggs' house, most of the cottages, and Cap'n Bill's stayed full. The Inn had more of a holiday atmosphere than Mr. Bragg's or the few other boarding houses. When the Inn could hold no more, Cap'n Bill became even busier, and friendlier, too.

Some of the young men who came to the pavilion and to the cottage were strangers. They had to get an introduction somehow, but that was not too hard to do. A first-time visitor could usually find a relative, a mutual friend, or some kind of connection in order to meet people at the dances or the cottages. After he was introduced, a new young man coming to our cottage still had to pass Mama's inspection. She invited the aspiring visitor to sit with her on the porch for a little while. She would smile and talk and learn all about him. Most passed; a few did not.

I never even saw one of the new visitors who caused a big commotion for our house party. He came to the square dance, not the cottage. He appeared and disappeared in one evening and we did not even know his name. I was trying to gig flounder along the shore at Springer's Point when it happened, and stopped by the pavilion just as our group was leaving. I heard all about him.

The dancers had finished a square set and the musicians were taking a short break. Mr. Jacobson, the leader, spoke to the accordian player hen announced a round dance was next. The man began to play "Carolina Moon." Sister came out on the floor with a boy from Rocky Mount who had been introduced by Cousin Helene. Mr. Jacobson stood back from the dancers with Wahab Howard and the caller, Sam Keech Williams, all drinking co'colas. Sister smiled at them as she danced by.

A young man who had been sitting by the door slowly crossed the floor, zigging around dancing couples and zagging around couples who were not there. He broke on Sister by tapping the boy from Rocky Mount on the shoulder; smiling at Sister he commenced to dance. Sister did not know the man, but she did not want to insult him by refusing to dance with him. She expected him to tell her he was somebody's cousin or somebody's guest.

It was not usual for strangers to break on ladies at the dances. But more was wrong than violated custom—the young man was drunk. He looked all right. He was well-dressed in an open collared, short-sleeved, white shirt, starched khaki trousers, and brown and white wing-tipped shoes. He had slicked-back sandy hair, and was very red-faced, like a beet with blond foliage. He could stand up, he could shuffle his feet around and he could grin, but he was drunk and he did not know it.

He felt exceptionally good, exceptionally happy, and wanted to beam joy to the world. He was full of rhythm and joy. He did not realize that his feet did not dance to the same beat as his internal rhythms but achieved only a slow shuffle. He knew he should tell Sister his name and that he was pleased to meet her. He formed the words in his head, but they would not come out right. He beamed at her and mumbled,"Yam, yam," deep in his throat. He wanted to tell her how glad he was to be dancing with the prettiest girl in the pavilion. He took a deep breath and tried again. "Yam, yam, yam," he gargled.

Sister was unbearably embarrassed but she did not know what to do. Some of the other couples noticed the man, and Mr. Jacobson called Wahab's attention to him. Before they could intervene, Aunt Lizzie sprang into action. She seldom came to the square dances, but if chaperonage required her, she attended.

The happy drunk suddenly became aware of a tall, grim-faced lady with hard black eyes standing beside him. He felt a hand on his shoulder as another hand firmly disengaged his own from Sister's. The grim lady spoke, "You should not be dancing with this young lady."

He was stunned. He shivered. "Yam, yam, Mam," he stammered. Lizzie, Sister and the Beet were the center of attention. Dancing ceased though the accordian player squeezed happily on. The man backed away from Lizzie. He backed across the dance floor. The dancers parted for him as the sea waters did for Moses and he backed out the door and out of sight. Sister, almost as red-faced as the drunk man had been, followed Lizzie to her seat. She was both embarrassed and angry. They sat in silence.

Mr. Jacobson signalled for another square dance, Sam Keech Williams announced it, and Wahab invited Sister to dance. She smiled wanly, thanked him, but said they were going. She and Aunt Lizzie left the pavilion just as I marched up carrying my gig (but no flounder). I fell in behind them with the rest of the girls tagging along after.

As soon as we left the dock, even before we had crossed the stile, Sister began to berate Aunt Lizzie. She really was outraged, which shocked me. I had never heard Sister talk to Aunt Lizzie the way she did then.

"Everybody on that dance floor was staring at me," she fumed, "You acted like I was a little baby. They were all looking at me. I wanted to fall through the floor."

Lizzie only said she thought it had been necessary, then withdrew into her shell. She had a hard shell. We walked down the beach in silence. The other girls hung back.

Sister began to fuss again. She burst into tears. She stopped, wheeled around and threw her arms around Aunt Lizzie's neck. She blubbered all over Lizzie's shoulder.

"I wanted you to come. Oh, Lizzie, I'm glad you got me. I didn't know what to do." She blubbered some more. The bright moonlight showed the incredibly sweet smile that Lizzie reserved for those she loved. She hugged Sister. I was satisfied that all was well again.

Everything was normal the next morning. The other girls were teasing Sister about "Brother Yam-Yam." Sister answered that if he could not dance very well, at least he did not talk too much.

Mary Bell, Mama's baby sister, was the youngest of the four McIlhenny girls. She was older than Sister and the other house-party girls, but she liked to square dance as much as they did. She was plump, with bobbed, dark-blonde hair, and big, blue eyes—the only blue eyes in a brown-eyed family, causing her brothers to nickname her "Blue." I called her Aunt Blue Bell.

I liked Aunt Mary Bell a lot. She was jolly and fun to be with, but she never stayed long, a week at the time was the most, because she was busy back home. She worked in an office downtown and supervised Bup's house-cleaning woman. Bup cooked for them, because Aunt Blue Bell was not very good at that. She also went out often at night.

Mr. Mayer, who enjoyed talking to all the ladies, specially liked to talk to Aunt Mary Bell. He was always very polite to Mama and Aunt Margaret and addressed them properly as

"Mrs." but Mary Bell he called by her given name. (If Mr. Mayer had a first name, I never heard it. It might have been Saladin.)

One evening Mr. Mayer said, "Mary Bell, you're altogether the wrong age." Aunt Mary Bell asked him what he meant by that. "Just what I said," he answered. "If you were ten years older, I'd want you to marry me. If you were ten years younger, I'd want you to marry my son Philip." Aunt Mary Bell came right back with, "Why Mr. Mayer, maybe I'd like to be an old man's darling." Everybody, including Mama, laughed. Mr. Mayer got up, saying, "Mary Bell, you're too quick-witted for me," and went home. I did not quite understand all that, but thought perhaps Aunt Mary Bell had done what that purple-pajamad widow had tried to do.

The one time Aunt Blue Bell disappointed me happened at the dance pavilion. I was wading around under the dock and pavilion searching for cool drink bottles for Cap'n Bill, who would reward me with a drink or a candy bar. I was wearing my tennis shoes because there were sharp shells and maybe broken bottles (Cap'n Bill wanted only whole ones). It was underwater beachcombing.

That night Aunt Mary Bell was talking to a man named Bill who had come off a yacht tied up at the end of the dock. They were standing right over my head, about half-way out on the dock. The man wanted her to get on his boat.

She said, "No, I will not go to that boat with you. Don't act like a fool. Are you going to tell me about your etchings next? I'm going back in the pavilion."

What are etchings? I wondered. Anyhow, that was not the answer I wanted Aunt Mary Bell to give. Night was not the time for a cruise, I agreed: you couldn't see anything. But I wanted her to say, "Why yes, we'll go out on the boat tomorrow, and my nephew Mac wants to come too."

Aunt Mary Bell's one fault was a lack of appreciation of boats!

BOATS

THE SHIPYARD WAS NOT AS BUSY in the later summers, although its work became more varied when I turned to other interests.

The cottage needed more ashtrays so Sister suggested to me that I make some from big scallop shells. We glued the scallop shell to a smaller clam shell, back to back, for a stable base. I found a large fish in an advanced state of ripeness on the shore, with its bones showing. I pulled loose some ribs shaped like chair rockers joined at one end. These were fastened with liquid solder to the bottom of a scallop shell. They would rock to and fro by themselves in a strong breeze. What advantage there was in a rocking ashtray, we did not know, but we preferred these Mark II models, and turned out dozens. The demand for ashtrays was soon exceeded by production.

Next we made what we called boomerangs from the slats of an old window blind I had brought home from the Doxsee house. We tacked two slats together in a cross and discovered that if we slung it skyward it whirled in a nice curve back toward the slinger. We hoped to perfect the boomerang and our technique so it would return to our hands.

None of these projects was really satisfying, though. We wanted *real* boats.

One morning I walked down to the shore right after breakfast. Glancing around, I spotted a strange, big boat at the end of Cap'n Bill's dock. She was bigger than the Washington boats and had a high cabin with a smokestack aft and a tall mast forward carrying a crow's nest. I had never seen a crow's nest before except in pictures. I scooted over to the dock and almost collided with Cap'n Bill who was hurrying ashore with an envelope and some papers in his hand.

"Cap'n Bill," I gasped, "what's that big old boat out there?"

"Menhaden trawler," the Cap'n muttered as he rushed past, "from the Bahamas."

Mr. Bragg and Julius had told me that the thick schools of little fish we sometimes saw were menhaden. Some of the other islanders had called them fatbacks and said they were full of oil and not worth a damn to eat. I was surprised that a big boat would come to catch them.

At the end of the dock I entered an invisible cloud that surrounded the trawler, almost thick enough to row through. It was the smell of fatbacks past, fatbacks present, and probably fatbacks future. I stayed, breathing the aroma and inspecting the boat. I hoped somebody would invite me aboard and let me climb the rope ladders, that actually had wooden steps, to the crow's nest.

I moved along the dock close enough to hear what the cluster of crewmen were saying. I was surprised at their soft, liquid speech, a part of which I could understand. It was mostly English that I heard, and then I realized from picture shows that it was a British accent. This was novel. I had never before heard black-skinned people talk like that. Nobody paid me any attention or invited me in their crow's nest, so I trotted back to the cottage to see if the others wanted to come hear this strange talk. They were still sitting around the table when I burst in.

"There's a great big trawler at Cap'n Bill's with a whole lot of colored people who talk like Englishmen. Come hear 'em," I panted.

Nobody wanted to go but Lee. Mama called after us to stay off that trawler. But we were too late. We saw the vessel leave the dock, turn, and head toward Portsmouth. We watched her dwindle away, enter the inlet, and head out to sea. No visit to a crow's nest for us.

For a moment I thought that I would build a crow's nest. I would start with a big barrel. On further consideration, I did not think I would—a crow's nest was not much good without a boat underneath it, after all.

I had heard some of the family talk about something called "Prohibition." Bup explained that it was a law to keep people from drinking any alcohol, but it did not work and people smuggled in things to drink, anyhow. Ships brought it ashore at Ocracoke and lots of other places.

My voyage must have happened before December 5, 1933, when Prohibition was officially repealed. I think it occurred in 1932 when I was eight years old, but it could have been earlier. The incident followed a strange quirk of the weather. The wind had not blown for two days. The Sound was a glassy sheet—a "flat ca'm" the fishermen called it. The ocean's surface was a slow, gentle roll, and even the inlet was almost placid.

One young islander, the owner of a twenty-five- or thirty-foot fishing boat, offered us a short cruise outside. (The Ocracokers referred to a voyage leaving the Sound and going out in the ocean as going "outside.") There was a large sailing vessel becalmed off shore, and he said he would take everybody out for a close inspection of her. The girls asked for Mama's approval and she agreed. She told me I could come, too. Neither Billy nor Lee was there for the event, and Mary Young scorned an unnecessary boat trip.

We all went out on Cap'n Bill's dock to board the boat. We cruised southwesterly along the shore, past Springer's Point and Teach's Hole, through the inlet and out into the ocean. Mama, in *de facto* command, sat in a deck chair in the cockpit with me under close control and the girls distributed around the boat. The captain at the wheel and his mate were in the small pilot house forward.

Distances over water are deceptive, even to an experienced Ocracoker, and the captain became worried about his gasoline supply, but the ship was closer than the land so he continued. When close enough he hailed the schooner and asked if they had any gasoline to spare. The answer, in heavily accented English, came back affirmative. They had some gas and would sell a few gallons.

The three-master proved to be Portuguese, or "Portagee" as the mate called it. It was the largest and handsomest ship I ever saw at Ocracoke. The captain of the schooner directed the captain of the gas boat to go around to the other side of the ship where there was a ladder and a hoist. The Ocracoke captain complied and the smaller vessel was made fast while the transaction was arranged. The schooner captain asked if anybody would like to come aboard while the fuel was transferred. I was crazy to get aboard a real ship. Mama agreed and the mate helped me and several of the girls up the ladder.

The long sweep of the decks, the immensely tall masts, the slow roll and creak of the spars were wonders to see and hear. The schooner's captain, who had put on his blue coat with brass buttons to receive his guests, looked just right. He lacked only a brass telescope under his arm to be perfect. It was as good as seeing Long John Silver himself. When Mrs. Silver, in more accented English, invited me aft to see their cabin, and showed me her pet parrot, I was so overwhelmed I was ready to sail to Portugal. Sister had to threaten to put me in irons to get me back in the gas boat.

After shouted thanks to the Portuguese captain, the party

started back to the island. The return was uneventful until we reached the inlet, where we were met by the Coast Guard cutter stationed on the island. When he saw the Coast Guard vessel approaching, the captain of the gas boat became worried about the number of life preservers on board. He sent the mate to bring out all that were in the cabin and to look for more in other places. Mama viewed the appearance of the Coast Guard with approval. Turning to Sister, she confided, "I knew there was no need to worry about running out of gas. The Coast Guard boys would take care of us. See, they're coming out to see if we need any help."

The United States Coast Guard, however, was not concerned about life preservers or gasoline. From their watchtower, the lookout had observed a small craft leave the island, go out to the schooner beyond the three mile limit, move around to the off-shore side, and load something. They were concerned about illegal liquor. They ordered the gas boat to stop, came alongside, and came aboard. The Chief, whom Mama knew, was cool, polite, and only mildly apologetic as he directed his men in the search. They looked in the cabin, under the bunks and seats, took up the floorboards, and removed the engine box. They searched every cubbyhole and cranny. The chief "seen his duty and he done it." They found nothing, of course. They let the subdued voyagers proceed.

Mama felt betrayed. All her strict rules, all her personal prohibition of drinking were for naught. Her chagrin and embarrassment were intense until she got mad about it, but that came later. The news of the search preceded our return to the cottage. The whole island knew before nightfall that "Miss Nita" had been suspected of rum-running. It was the best joke of the season to everybody but Mama.

Not everyone was brave enough to ask her about it. To those who did, she answered dryly, "The Chief did his duty as he saw it." She had no answer for all the knowing grins that greeted her.

A few close friends asked if she was considering a new career. Even Pa heard about it in time to send a message by a passenger on the next boat, that if she wanted a drink that badly, next time let him know. Mama was not amused by any of the remarks, but she got through it. And she never relaxed her rule about drinking at the cottage.

The Chief told Mama later, "Miss Nita, when I saw you I knew there was no liquor aboard, but if I hadn't searched and anybody on the island got drunk that night, some fools would of said Nita McIlhenny brought some in."

Both Lee and I wanted a rowboat of our own, but we knew we did not have the skill or the right materials to build one. I had talked to Bup a lot about boat building and hoped he would help me build one someday.

In our rambles around the island, we had seen some boats that might be a step between the toy boats we had built and the full-sized skiff we wanted. On porches and under sheds we had seen several little skiffs, about four feet long, just sitting there unused. We examined one under a shed. It was built just like a real skiff, but with cross braces instead of seats. We tried speculation and deductive reasoning to determine the use of the little boats. The boats were too little for us to get into and we did not believe that even Ocracoke babies had their own boats. Besides, the boats had no seats nor oars. Lee said they might be models people built before they built a big skiff. We rejected that idea because we thought a man building a big skiff could just copy another one. The simple solution was to ask one of the Ocracokers, but we were reluctant to appear ignorant.

The mystery was not solved when Brother Sammy and Cousin Tommy came for the weekend. I walked 'round the Creek with them and risked asking the question when we passed the little boat in the shed. I was soon sorry I had asked.

"Why it's a training boat for little kids," Sammy told me.

"They start 'em early on the island." When I asked about seats and oars, Sammy answered that the boat was not finished.

Cousin Tommy joined in and said the islanders held junior boat races every year, a big event. "I've been to the race. They call it the Three-Year-Old Regatta and give a big prize to the winner." I knew they were teasing, but had to ask what was the prize. "A sterling silver combination chamber pot and boat bailer," Tommy told me. Luckily, the big boys were distracted by some girls and left me alone, relieved, but no wiser.

We solved the mystery by observation a few days later. We were exploring the shore past the Coast Guard Station, around the point and along the shore of a place called Mary Ann's Pond. A man was out on the sand bar raking clams with one of the little boats tethered behind him. As he raked in some clams he dumped them in the little boat. When it was loaded, he transferred the clams to his big skiff which was anchored nearby. He poled the big skiff further down the sandbar, anchored, and started raking again, and towing the little skiff. Elizabeth O'Neal confirmed that the boat's correct name was simply clam boat.

I did not know it at the time, but the little clam boat was a perfect example of form following function as were the shad boat and the bugeye oyster schooner. The clam boat was light in the water and easier to tow than a box would have been. It was more stable and seaworthy than a wash tub. Whatever its form and function, we decided we had to have one.

We developed a good prospect for one of the boats in old Mr. Credle who lived in a little house on the road behind Mr. Bragg's. He had a clam boat upside down on his back porch and he looked too old to go clamming. I had previously met him when I helped carry a bucket of well water to his house. His pump had "give out," Mr. Credle said and he hauled drinking water from a neighbor's pump. Lee and I had twice done him this service.

We discussed the best method of parting Mr. Credle from his clam boat. We realized a few buckets of water did not make much of a claim, so we resolved to try a direct approach to determine how highly Mr. Credle valued the boat. Lee had seventy-five cents left of his month's spending money and I had a quarter, but thought I could raise fifty cents more from Sister or Mama.

We just happened to be strolling by his house that afternoon and saw the old man in his backyard. "Hey, Mr. Credle. Wha'cha doin'? Need some water?" I asked.

"No, much obliged", he answered, "buckets're full."

Lee ambled over to the clam boat, I followed. "Mr. Credle," Lee asked, "How much would you take for this old boat? Ain't it in your way?"

"Yeah—yessir, maybe we'd want to buy it," I added. "Take it off your porch."

"Well, I don't know about sellin' it, boys. My grandson might ever want it. He used to like to set in it when he was little. He's about your size now. Comin' with my daughter next week and I'll ast him about it. They're from Ahoskie. I'm gonna stay with 'em next winter, mebby. Gettin' too old to live here all the time. We'll see, boys, we'll see." Mr. Credle started in the house. "Goin' to lie down a spell, now. Stop by any time, boys."

We trudged home to try to salvage our wrecked plan.

"Maybe his grandson won't want it. What did he say his name was?" I asked.

"I don't think he said," Lee answered. "Where is Ahoskie anyhow? Do they have clams there?"

"I bet it's in the mountains somewhere. Prob'ly don't even have any water there. I know one thing," I grumbled, "I wouldn't want to live in a place called Ahoskie." We jumped in the Sound to wash away our frustration.

That afternoon, Mr. Mayer paid a brief, post-fishing call. He brought a big seafood bouquet, a bucket stuffed with puppy drum, heads down, tails in the air. Mr. Mayer's brisk pace jiggled the bucket so the finny fish tails waved in the air like flowers in the wind. There were enough and more for a fried fish supper.

Mama and Mary Young took over the bouquet and put it on the back porch shelf. Mama told us, "Come back here in an hour. I'll want you all to get rid of the fish scraps." She and Mary Young disappeared in the kitchen to get pans and knives and things.

I quickly abstracted the biggest fish from the bucket and called Lee, "Let's go see Mr. Credle." The plan to overwhelm Mr. Credle with goodness was still in effect, grandson or no.

Mr. Credle was rocking on his front porch. I greeted him, "Hey Mr. Credle, want a puppy drum for supper? We got lots of 'em."

Lee added, "He's right fresh. We got a bucketful."

"Why thank ye, boys. Best frying fish there is. You been out in the Sound?"

"Nossir—" I started.

Lee chimed in with, "—Mostly we fish from Mr. Bragg's pier." Neither of us considered that lying; it was only misleading. "Want us to clean him, Mr. Credle?"

"No, thank ye. Can still do some things meself. Come around back. And ye' caught 'im from Gary's pier, eh?" The old man creaked to his feet and started through the house. "Rheumatiz is bad in my laigs today."

He met us at his fish-cleaning table in the back yard, carrying a slim-bladed knife, a heavy-bladed knife, and a pan. The knives' cutting edges glittered. He braced one leg against the table and pointed to the fish, "Give it here, will you?" His legs were stiff, but nothing was wrong with his arms and hands. Mr. Credle showed us what fish cleaning was all about. First one knife, then the other flickered and flashed. A jeweled cascade of fish scales glistened in the sun as they showered on the grass. Fast beyond belief, two nice puppy drum fillets were lying in the pan and Mr. Credle was wiping his knives clean on a fig leaf. "Boys," he asked us, "will ye throw those scraps unded the fig bush? For me cats."

Our discussion of lightning-fish-cleaning ended at the cottage when Mama handed me the bucket of fish scraps. "Empty this. Rinse it and scrub it with sand—thoroughly. Take it back to Mr. Mayer or Gary Bragg, then come right back to supper." We ate all the fried puppy drum we could hold.

Mr. Credle and clam boats hung in our minds and surfaced occasionally during the rest of the week, but we did not visit him. On Monday, however, Mr. Credle had company on his porch: a grown lady, well dressed, and a boy our age, pale-faced and red-headed.

Mr. Credle called us in, saying to the lady, "These here are the boys who hep me tote water. They're gettin' to be fishermen, too."

"Hello, boys," the lady said. "You're Mac and you're Lee?" she asked, getting it right. "Thank you for helping Papa." She did not sound much like an Ocracoker. "I told Harold somebody his age would be here. He hasn't visited Papa since he was a little fellow, and doesn't know anybody. Harold, speak to the boys."

Harold scowled and grunted, "Hi! You live here?"

Extending our goodness program even to Harold, we explained, "We come in the summer and stay in the McIlhenny cottage. Want to go swimmin' or go down to the beach with us?"

Harold jumped off the porch, said he did not care much for swimming and asked where was the beach. "Be back for supper!" his mother called.

"You play any baseball?" Harold demanded. "Where do you play at?"

We did not play any baseball at Ocracoke. We liked to swim and fish and explore.

"We do some clammin'," Lee answered.

"Climbin'? Climbin' what?" Harold asked.

"No, *clammin'*. Rakin' for clams on the sand shoal," we explained further.

"Sounds like a dumb thing to do," Harold sneered.

His answer pleased us so much that we told him the island boys sometimes played baseball in the school yard.

"Less go by the Doxsee House and then 'round the Creek," I suggested, thinking Harold might want a geography lesson.

Harold wanted to know what was at the "Dossy" house and was the Creek the place they had got off the mail boat. After we answered, he did not want to visit either place. "Show me the schoolhouse," he ordered. We faltered through a conversation on the way to the school. Nobody was there. Harold wanted to return to his grandfather's house and Lee and I were glad to guide him. As we hiked back to the cottage we analysed Harold in a way that would not have pleased him. However, we approved of his attitude toward clamming. Our clam-boat plan looked hopeful.

Next day, just for Mr. Credle, we tried once more to entertain Harold. He was on the front porch again, and as soon as he saw us he accused us of spreading disinformation. "There wasn't anybody at that schoolhouse this morning. I went and looked."

We invited him to come with us to Cap'n Bill's for a cool drink. Harold allowed himself to be persuaded, so we all started back to the Sound shore.

"Don't cha want to take off your shoes?" I asked.

"No," Harold snapped, "I don't. The sand's too hot. I tried it yesterday." Lee and I just smiled at the tenderfoot, not mentioning that we, too, had suffered through hot sand, especially on the way to the ocean. I had often stood in a tiny patch of shade one legged, like a crane, alternately cooling each foot.

We led Harold past Bup's cottage, across the Turtle Ditch, and out on the Sound shore. We talked about the island and boats, Harold talking about baseball, nobody listening. I started running toward the Inn, past several skiffs pulled up on shore. Harold followed, Lee brought up the rear. As Harold clumped past the bow of a skiff, he tripped over the anchor half buried in the sand, and plowed a furrow with his chin. He scrambled to his feet, rubbed his chin, and turned in fury to see what had tripped him.

"Thass it," he pointed. "I fell over that dam' ankelor. Who put it there?"

I was delighted. "That what?"

"It's an *anchor*," Lee grinned.

"That's what I said! A ankelor!" Harold yelled, "People hadn't ought to leave ankelors layin' around like that."

Harold fussed and grumbled about stray ankelors the whole time we were in the pavilion drinking soda pop. He would not even go to the end of the dock to inspect a new gas boat moored there.

We escorted Harold home and did not see him but once more. A boy who did not like swimming, or fishing, or boats was not worth our time, especially one who talked about ankelors. We felt a little bit sorry for Mr. Credle.

Early on Friday morning we helped Cousin Glenmore and Howard tote their suitcases out on Mr. Bragg's pier. They were going home on the mailboat to Atlantic. The mailboat left her dock in the Creek at six o'clock, but she would stop at the two Sound-shore piers to pick up more passengers. The *Aleta* made the early morning voyage to Atlantic six days a week and returned to Ocracoke in late afternoon. She was smaller than the Washington boat and had no sails, but it was a nice trip anyway. Passengers could sit in the long cabin or on top of the cabin under an awning. I had come that way once, but did not remember why.

We helped Glenmore load her cases, then looked over the mailboat. On the top deck, under the awning, were most of the Creek passengers, among them Harold and his mother. She waved to us; we waved back. Harold nodded when we yelled, "Bye Harold. Look out for ankelors!" He stuck his tongue out.

As the mailboat churned away, stern to the dock, a horrid sight was revealed. On the stern deck, lashed to the rail, was Mr.

Credle's clam boat. We were aghast. Harold, who thought clam-ming was dumb, had taken it.

We ate breakfast muttering to each other about bat-brained Harold, with feet like soft crabs. When Mama asked us what was wrong, we lied, "Oh, nothing." "Eat your breakfast then and stop whispering about nothing."

We decided to go to Mr. Credle's house to show him we were not mad with him and to maybe ask him who else had a clam boat. Mr. Credle saw us on the porch at the screen door and beck-oned us into the kitchen. He was propped against the sink wash-ing a pan full of dishes.

"I got me pump fixed, boys. No more water hauling. I'm sorry about the clam boat. Harold decided he wanted it. But come on out back. I've got somethin' for ye'."

The old man hobbled around to his shed and pulled out a clam rake. "Take this," he said. "Mebbe you kin find a boat somers else, I dunno. I've got two rakes, one for you all and one for Simey. I'll not be needin' them. Next year I be movin' in with my daughter to stay."

We were truly sorry for Mr. Credle having to leave Ocracoke and tried to tell him so. We took the clam rake with many thanks. Lee asked Mr. Credle if Harold would rake clams at Ahoskie.

"You know not," Mr. Credle chuckled, "Not even a creek there that I ever heered of. Harold said he wanted to keep his baseball things in the wee boat."

We were *really* sorry for Mr. Credle then. The poor old man had a sissy grandson who talked about ankelors and kept base-ball bats in a clam boat. He deserved to live in the mountains at Ahoskie, but poor Mr. Credle did not.

DEMONS

THE DOXSEE HOUSE remained an interesting place to visit, or the source of a special board for the ship yard, but it had lost its spookiness. Lee and I had carried little Wheeler there to scare him away from us, but that did not work. Wheeler just asked if the place was for rent. As a haunted house, it needed internal improvements.

My new friend Johnny was a semi-Ocracoker who spent summers on the island with his aunt and uncle. I had seen him before, but we had become buddies only this summer. We discussed grave robbing and, though we were not serious about doing it, we somehow enjoyed talking about it.

"What we need is a skellerton," Johnny offered as we left the Doxsee house. "It's an okay haunted house, but we got to fix it up scaryier."

I had an idea, "Maybe we could *build* a skellerton. Use some goat bones or some pony bones and build a big one." Skeet Howard's hog's head flashed before my eyes.

I was Skeets Howard's elder by two or three years, and as such considered him just a nice little kid. He had kin folk on the island and was a regular summer visitor, but I was not around him much. Skeets was sick that summer and I accompanied Mama to visit him and his mother. To entice him to eat, Miss Rita offered to get anything he wanted. Of all things possible, Skeets wanted a hog head. There was not one on the island, so Miss Rita ordered one through Captain Dave on the *Preston* and Mr. Howard in Washington. It came on the next boat—a corned hog head in a wooden tub. Miss Rita cooked it and Skeets picked at it until it was gone. I did not like its looks, but pulled off a strip when Skeets offered it. It was tasty even if it looked fierce.

The memory of Skeets' hog head reminded me of another skull. "I know, I know! I know where we can get a monster skull maybe."

The need to improve the Doxsee house was caused by our acquaintance with two new visitors to the island. Jack and Bill, professional Virginians from Norfolk, liked to bragg about the superiority of all things in Virginia. Virginia's beaches were nicer, her fish were bigger, and Chesapeake Bay was better than Pamlico Sound. When the talk turned to boats, the Virginians displayed the whole U.S. Navy, battleships, submarines, and all. We had no answers to that, but wanted to get even. Maybe we could scare them.

We hurried along the Sound shore to Springer's Point, and turned inland toward the ocean. I remembered finding a goat's skull one previous summer. Billy had theorized to me about what kind of horned creature had owned it. Of all the things he named, I remembered the "Great Horned Eel" best, even though we knew it was a goat. After several hours of hot, dry, pleasant exploration, we found it. Old horny was still there, half buried in the sand, awaiting its ordained use.

We carried the treasure back to the Doxsee house, trying to avoid people and houses along the way. One islander asked us with a grin, "Are ye lookin' for the rest of y'r billy-goat?" We deposited the skull under the house and retired to the edge of the Creek to perfect our plan. Sitting on a timber with our feet in the water was conducive to clear thinking. We were soon ready.

We began to gather the props we needed for our "monster haint." The collecting took the rest of the day, so we began assembly the next morning in a dark back room of the Doxsee house. A back attic furnished us a tattered dress maker's form and a box for a seat. I found several yards of black cloth in Uncle Joe's hidey-hole in our cottage. Johnny brought fishing line, wire, and a pair of pliers. We sat the form on the box and tied the skull on top, and wrapped it in Uncle Joe's black cloth. We put a shattered fish box that we found on the shore in front of it. We thought we were unobserved as we worked away.

Mama was all smiles at the supper table that night. Brother Sammy had come that morning for a short visit. His friends Clark and Owen had come with him to visit their family's cottage. Next morning, Johnny and I inspected our monster one last time. It was a fearful sight, with the skull leering atop a black-swathed body. We set off to find Jack and Bill and to elicit a dare from them to visit the Doxsee house at night.

We gathered on the shore after dark. Johnny led the way into the old house, urging the Virginians on with a weak flashlight. The plan was for me to scream and howl as soon as Johnny flashed his light on the monster. But as soon as we entered the room, before I could scream, something roared and stomped and shook the house. Johnny and the visitors flew out the front door, I jumped out a window and lit running. I do not know who won the race to get out first. When I stopped to catch my breath, I saw three shadows leave the back of the house, one of them very large. Brother Sammy had ruined our plot.

Big brothers as big as Sammy, as fast moving, and as quick tempered, were hard to deal with. The Lord, however had shown David how to handle Goliath. I did not want to really hurt Sammy, but it would be nice to torture him just a little. A chance for retribution came later in the month.

Sammy, along with Clark and Owen, came for another weekend. I had to endure more jibes from the older boys, but the misery was short-lived, for they were interested in girls, not ghosts.

I walked alone that afternoon, past Cap'n Bill's and on toward Springer's Point, musing about all sorts of things, including big brothers. A shout from ahead snapped me out of my reverie and I looked up to see Sammy, Clark, and Owen cavorting out in the water just around the point. It was a place I too used to go swimming "nekkid." I quickly turned inland, for they had not seen me.

I slipped through the brush until I intersected the road to Mr. Springer's house and walked past it in the shelter of the big trees. I turned again and crept through the bushes, still unobserved. I spied the big boys' clothing hung on bushes next to the beach. Some of their clothes had blown off the bushes—a shirt and all three pairs of under shorts lay on the sandy beach.

I crawled closer and watched them, wishing for some itching powder or something. I considered looking for poison ivy to rub in their drawers, but rejected that as too drastic. I remembered my buddy Jim Filling lying in bed in his pajama top with his bottom parts painted with pink chalk. It took old Jim about a week to get over his case of poison ivy.

I squirmed and shifted under the bush, for I was crouched in a nest of sand spurs. The solution became clear! I harvested a handful of sand spurs and carefully, carefully crept out of the bushes to sprinkle them generously in the underwear pants. I had just withdrawn to the bushes when the big boys shouted something and rushed ashore to throw on their clothes. From their vantage point out in the water, they had seen the house-party girls strolling toward them.

The boys just had time to dress and assume their usual non-chalance toward girls when the two groups met, merged, and chattered away. They all turned and marched back toward the Inn. Sammy had a crush on Cousin Helene that summer. I saw him put his arm around her—with his other hand he started tugging at the seat of his pants. He did a quick little sideways hop, still tugging, and released Cousin Helene. She tittered and asked him what was wrong. I could not hear his answer, but I saw Clark drop behind the others and yank the seat of his pants with both hands. Only Owen seemed to be immune to sand spurs.

I shifted to a more comfortable spot, lay back and enjoyed my thoughts and the breeze. Someone did look out for little brothers after all. Silence, I concluded, was my best course. Later on I heard that Sammy and Clark had a fight. I wondered if sand spurs were responsible for that.

The one good result of all our work building the haint for the failed monster plot was an exploration I had deferred. From the top of the sand dune where we re-found the goat skull, I saw the swimming hole I had observed previously from Cap'n Bill's beach truck. It was behind Springer's Point and about half way to the ocean. Some of the island boys went swimming and diving there, but I had never swum in it. Johnny did not even know about the place, so we had to investigate.

We were the only swimmers there, so we jumped right into our private swimming hole. It was disappointing. I expected the water to be fresh, but it was brackish. It was also warm. Compared to the Sound, it was like being in a tin bathtub, and I could not understand why the Ocracoke boys swam there. I asked one boy, who answered, "Hit was there, so we used it."

SIGNALS & SMOKE

THE SUMMER of the Portuguese Bottle Mail Service is one of the few summers whose events I can date exactly. Lee kept a letter his sister Marjorie wrote to him at Ocracoke asking about the island. It is dated July, 1934. Though we had no inkling of it at the time, this was to be Lee's last summer on the island. The next summer he would visit his mother's family in New Orleans.

Our established custom on the first day we arrived on the island was a tour of the Sound shore to check on old friends and to look for changes.

As soon as we could escape from unloading and baggage handling, Lee and I took off for the Pamlico Inn. We knew about the fire the previous August and wanted to look at the damage. Back home we had heard many stories about the fire: wild confusion at first, people running out of the wrong rooms, and both islanders and guests fighting the flames. We had seen from the deck of the Washington boat the new coat of white paint, but no other changes. We could see one other sign when we crossed the stile: a section of bright, shiny, new tin roof on the front of the wing nearest Springer's Point.

On the way to the Inn we met Johnny, who had been there that night and he told about what he saw. The fire had started late at night. Somebody roused Cap'n Bill, who got everybody out of that wing. He sent word to all the Gaskills and the Gaskins and formed a bucket brigade. In a short while most of the Ocracokers on the Pointer side of the island came to help. Johnny came with his uncle and cousins. They contained the fire and finally managed to put it out, with only two rooms burned out. They spent the rest of the night drinking coffee and talking about the fire. Drinking some other stuff, too, Johnny added.

I told Johnny a story I had heard in Washington. A Washingtonian named Mr. Murdock rushed out of one of the rooms along with the lady who lived there. She quickly joined friends in another room. Mr. Murdock, wearing flame-red silk pajamas, dashed along the second floor porch, down the stairs, and across the courtyard to his own room, where his wife, who was deaf, was still asleep. Mr. Murdock then joined the firefighters and managed to retrieve the bathrobe he had dropped on the upstairs porch.

The Washington gossip said the fire was started by Mr. Murdock's red hot pajamas. Mrs. Murdock told people that her husband had ruined an almost new bathrobe beating out sparks with it. He wanted to do his part, she said.

Johnny recollected he had seen the red-pajamed man walking around in a ratty looking wet bathrobe. He did not know how the fire started. Some of the Ocracokers thought maybe an oil lamp had ignited a curtain. The fire demonstrated to Lee and me how the Ocracokers rallied in an emergency to help each other. It was a good lesson to learn.

I knew Mr. Murdock in later years: a dignified, portly, white-haired, old gentleman, most often spending his time entertaining his grandchildren, nieces, and nephews. I still visualized him walking around in red silk pajamas looking for his bathrobe.

Our tour continued as we walked past Springer's Point, wheeled around and back-tracked past the Inn toward the Doxee house. At the high tide line near Aunt Ella's cottage I spotted a super bottle: clear glass with a big coat of arms and some curly-cues cast in it, and the words *Agua de Solares*. It was worth taking home.

Mama and the girls had stopped unpacking and were eating lunch. I put the bottle on the table and told Mama I had brought Johnny to lunch because we had to do a lot of planning that afternoon. Mama smiled at Johnny and said, "Go to it, boys. Make your own sandwiches."

Wookie examined the bottle and told me the word Agua meant water in Spanish and, she thought, in Portuguese, too. Solares had something to do with the sun. She translated it as "Water of the Sun." The other girls said it meant very strong drink. I gave the bottle to Wookie, but she said it was so pretty they ought to use it for a vase in the cottage. She put some Joe Bell flowers in it that afternoon. I was in love with Wookie. If I could not give my lady friends diamonds and rubies, at least I could find fancy bottles for them.

The talk at the supper table turned to bottles, as the new one was prominent on the table. The girls could make funny jokes on any subject—including messages in bottles. The idea took root, and the Portuguese Bottle Mail Service was born.

Lee and I collected a supply of suitable bottles along the shore and began to compose suitable notes. The first mailings were treasure maps roughly plagiarized from *Treasure Island*. Lee's map resembled Ocracoke, while mine was what I thought Indian Island looked like. The next series of bottles contained letters purporting to come from castaway sailors offering rewards for their rescue.

The mail service ran short of corks, as most castaway bottles lacked them, so we whittled sticks to fill the need. Next, the bottles gave out. The final dispatch of the Portuguese Bottle Mail Service was a note from each one of us giving his name and address with a request that the finder let us know where he picked up the bottle. These were scientifically sealed by candle wax dribbled over the cork. Before casting the final bottles into the Sound, we threw sticks overboard to make certain that the tide was going out. While we pursued other interests, the tide turned.

I got an answer to my letter after school opened that fall. Pa brought it to me from the post office, a typed envelope postmarked New York. I opened it carefully, wondering who could have written me such an official-looking letter. Folded in a letter neatly typed on thick cream colored paper was one of my bottle notes. It was the last one, identified by spots of wax.

I postponed reading the letter for a few moments, prolonging the suspense and savouring the moment. I recollected sending the bottle mail, and when I could stand it no longer I unfolded the letter. It read:

> *4900 Park Avenue*
> *New York City*
> *September 15, 1934*

Dear Sir:

> *While cruising in my yacht off the northwest coast of Cuba a short time ago, I picked up a floating bottle.*

> *I had seen something glinting in the sun and had called it to the captain's attention. I ordered a deckhand to pick it up and bring it to me on the bridge. The bottle contained your note, which is enclosed herewith.*

> *With all good wishes to you, I remain,*
> > *Yours truly,*
> > *J. Reginald Swillingham III*

I was as surprised as I was jubilant. I bolted out the door and tore around to Lee's house. Lee, who was both interested and envious, waited in vain for an answer to his Bottle Mail. We agreed that Mr. Swillingham Three must be a nice man to take time to answer the note, but one part of his letter worried us: when he wrote, "I ordered a deck hand to pick it up," he sounded so stuck-up. We rationalized the matter by deciding that was just the way Yankee yacht owners talked. We even adopted the words for ourselves sometimes, so that if one of us expressed a wish for something, the other retorted, "Have your deckhand pick it up for you." I soon learned that nobody else was very interested in my bottle mail, so I quit talking about it.

I did not tell anybody, not even Lee, that I had mailed a thank you note to Mr. Swillingham Three. I invited my correspondent to cruise to Ocracoke next year and offered to show him around the island if Mr. Swillingham would order his deckhand to come to the McIlhenny cottage to get me. I never received an answer.

For a good reason. Brother Sammy told me, though not until next spring, that the letter was a joke. Clark and Owen's brother Archie had found the bottle washed ashore near Springer's Point. He decided to have some fun, so he typed the letter and gave it to a friend to mail from New York. "You were having too much fun with that letter," Sammy laughed, "for me to tell you about it then." I did not think it was such a good joke, because I worried about some stranger from 4900 Park Avenue showing up at Ocracoke. Nobody ever came that I heard of.

I discovered another change at the Pamlico Inn the summer after the fire, something not obvious, but useful. Cap'n Bill had installed a new piling cap along one side of the pavilion. The timber stuck out a few inches, making a narrow shelf I could just shuffle along with my body flattened against the wall. I could ease along the side and look in the windows unobserved. The only hazard was falling overboard, but I never minded that.

One morning's shelf-shuffle rewarded me with a private view of Jim Baugham Gaskill and Sister Mary. Jim Baugham, who was cleaning the snack bar all alone, had opened a box of cigars and lit one. He was puffing and blowing smoke like a fat-back trawler when Sister strolled in. Gallantly, he offered her one; impulsively she took it, surprising all three of us. They both puffed away to my mute amazement. Jim Baugham began to turn pale, but could not stop puffing in front of a girl. Sister had enough, too. They were saved when Miss Annie Gaskill stormed in.

"Jim Baugham," she roared, "take that thing out of your mouth. You can't smoke seegars. Usin' up stock, too. Just wait till I tell the Captain." She snatched the cigar from his hand. She confronted Sister a little less ferociously. "You make a pretty picture with that thing, Mary Mallison. What will your mother think? What will Miss Lizzie say about you smokin' a seegar?"

"Yes, M'am, Miss Annie. I better go now." Sister threw her cigar right past my head outside the window and never saw me. She slipped out as Miss Annie turned back to Jim Baugham.

I slid back to the dock without falling overboard and followed Sister. I had no intention of telling Mama or Lizzie, but thought I would tease Sister awhile. After further consideration, I decided that perhaps Sister might think throwing me off the dock was not enough, so I said nothing.

BATHS & BODIES

I SAT IN THE MORNING SUNSHINE, replete with eggs, fish, and biscuits, gazing at everything and nothing. As I shifted my vision from a Down-Below direction to look at Pointer Beach and Portsmouth, I almost fell off the pier with surprise. I saw a boat close in, heading for the Creek entrance. It looked like an oyster boat, a one-masted sail boat, the kind people called a skipjack. Bup had said it could also be called a bateau and spelled it for me. This one had what looked like boards piled on the deck. I decided to investigate as soon as I could, but first I had to follow Evelyn and Gladys.

I knew where they were going by the little bundles they carried. They headed for the Pamlico Inn to use the showers, for they hardly ever used the big tin bathtub in the girls' room. (I had always thought that bathtub was a crazy idea with all the good swimming water at Ocracoke.) They usually showered about midmorning when the bathrooms were not busy. I watched the girls go to the ladies' shower room, with one of them peeping out on lookout. They did not want Cap'n Bill or Miss Annie to see them.

I sat on the big brick cistern in the courtyard and waited. Only a few guests populated the pier, pavilion, and porches. The fishermen were out in the Sound and the beach truck had just chugged off for the ocean. Cap'n Bill strode out from the dining room, glanced over at the shower room, nodded to me, and headed for the dock. Charlotte, the lookout, dodged back in the door. I knew Cap'n Bill had seen the girls and he did not seem to care. I decided to talk to Sister about that.

I idled back to the cottage just in time for Mama to catch me for a water-hauling trip to Mr. Ballance's pump. When I finished that chore it was lunch time, so I did not get 'round the Creek to inspect the new sail boat until afternoon.

I escaped from the cottage and spotted the new sailboat at the big dock near the entrance. I broke into the hopping-trot I reserved for urgent matters. Two men were loading the last of the boards on a big flatbed truck. The captain of the ship, the *Janie* of Engelhard, N.C., hollered something at his two men about getting back fast. One of them was half-fat and red-headed and the other one was skinny and black-headed. A couple of boards fell off the truck as the driver started to move. I jumped forward and helped reload the boards. The truck groaned off through the sand.

Even though the skipjack's captain had been glaring and yelling at his crew, I risked asking him if I could come aboard. The captain smiled and said, "Sure. Come aboard, son."

I peered down the open hatch at the empty hold. The captain told me the lumber was going to Stanley Wahab's new building project, and that he had another cargo to load as soon as his two lazy scoundrels came back. "We got to shove off," he said, "to make the train." I did not know what that meant, but the captain's next words really surprised me. "Boy, do ye' want to sign on the *Janie* for a v'yage to Washin'ton?"

I did not understand whether he was joking or not, but answered the same way. "

"Yes sir, I do. I'll have to go tell my mother where I've gone to first. Be right back."

The captain shook his head, "Might not be time, son, might not be time." He disappeared into his cabin.

I trailed the truck to the building site. The two men from the *Janie* stood talking to some other men by the unloaded truck. The other men went back to work on a building, and the two *Janie* men strolled away. They did not hurry, I noted. Bup would have said they were lollygagging. The other building on the site was the new dance hall, which I had not seen since it was finished. I looked inside where everything was clean and shiny, but no people were there. The house-party girls had been there for square dances two or three times. Sister had told me the floor was better than the floor in Cap'n Bill's pavilion, but they liked the dances at Cap'n Bill's better. The pavilion out over the water was cooler and Mr. Jacobson's music was better. I added to myself that Zoph's piano playing was better too, before he ate too much.

I loped toward the Creek to check the *Janie* again, but slowed when I saw the *Janie* men in a little grove of trees. Carrot Top and Black Hair were sitting on a timber passing a bottle back and forth between them. I could smell it where I stood, and they were not preserving frogs with it. They were red-faced and laughing as they guzzled from the bottle. Blackie tossed the empty bottle away, they stopped laughing and jumped up. I could not hear exactly what they said, but they were fussing. Carrot Top pushed Black Hair and they fell to fighting. Carrot Top knocked Blackie down. Blackie staggered to his feet, seized a two by four from the ground, swung it like a base ball bat, and slammed Carrot Top on the side of his head. Carrot Top thumped on the ground, head bloody, as still as an anchor, and Blackie ran off through the woods.

I rushed over to kneel by the body and put my hand on his back. Carrot Top did not move, did not make a sound. I was sure he was dead and realized I was the only witness to a crime. I remembered a detective story I had read, about a killer stalking a witness to shut him up. I jumped up, looked all around for

Blackie, then took off, running as fast as I could for home. I hardly slowed, except to look back over my shoulder. I wanted to talk to somebody about what to do. I collapsed on the porch of the cottage and found nobody home. I wanted advice, but did not know who to ask. I needed to see Daddy or Bup, not the house-party girls or Mama for this.

I slipped in to the dark little back room and sat on the bed to worry. I wanted to talk to a man, but could not think of the right one. I heard someone out in the road. Was it Blackie? I recognized Mr. Bragg's and Julius's voices. I started outside. Mr. Bragg was walking toward his house, Julius toward the pier. Julius had that great big pocket knife, a good weapon.

"Hey, Julius, wait a minute.

"Julius," I blurted, "Whut would you do if you saw a man kill another man?"

Julius stopped, stared at me. "Whut you talkin' about, Mac?"

I gobbled out an account of the fight.

"How you know he was daid?" Julius demanded.

"He didn't move none or breathe. His head was all bloody."

" Huh! Whut you seen was a fight. Bes' thing ye can do is to keep yo' mouth shut." Julius was not convinced there had been a killing, but I was. I wanted company.

"Where you goin', Julius? Can I come with you?"

"Goin' to Mr. Gary's fish house wid the skiff. Come on."

Julius poled the skiff while I huddled on the seat and worried. I would not have walked 'round the Creek for fear of seeing Blackie, but the skiff and fish house seemed safe. Julius moored the skiff and went inside to bring out some kegs of fish which he lined up on the edge of the dock. "Six tubs of corned mullet," Julius told me, "He'p me lift 'em down in the skiff." I asked if they were taking the fish back to Mr. Bragg's. "No", Julius said, "We takin' 'em over to that oysterman", and pointed to the *Janie* across the Creek.

"No", I hollered, "I don't want to go there!"

Julius just rowed on. I thought of jumping overboard. I spotted an old, raggedy straw hat under a seat and put it on as a disguise. It fitted down over my ears, more of a hiding place than disguise. As we drew close to the *Janie,* a truck with more fish kegs backed to the dockside. The captain called down the hatch, "Here's the rest of 'em." A man climbed out of the hatch. To my horror it was Blackie. I climbed further in my hat, watching Blackie as a charmed bird watches a snake. But what was this? Climbing after Blackie came Carrot Top, a rag tied around his head. Julius had been right; nobody was dead. I burst out laughing so hard in relief that Julius cut his eyes around and glared to make me stop. Blackie and Carrot Top were not dead, but they looked half-dead. Each one was as white faced as a seasick highland terrapin and dripping sweat.

"Get those off the truck. These are the last ones." Then to Julius, "These from Gary Bragg? Put 'em on deck there. I'll send 'em below." He handed Julius a paper. He hollered at his crew again. "Look lively. Wind's fair and we can sail her out and get to Washin'ton with these-here mullet. Ye can rest one at the time on the way across. There's some black coffee in the pot. Look lively."

The *Janie,* carrying the living and the half-dead, had swanned out of the Creek by the time the skiff reached Mr. Bragg's pier. Blackie was slumped down by the captain aft. Carrot Top was flat out again on the hatch cover. I watched them sail far out in the Sound.

Next morning, after my first swim, two of the girls left with their towel bundles, heading for the Inn's showers. I resolved to talk to Sister about Cap'n Bill and the showers that very night, but so much happened that I forgot all about it again.

A family had recently arrived at the Nunnelee cottage. There were three boys, ranging from younger-than to older-than me, who looked sort of familiar. The girl in the family, about Sister's age, was pretty. In my new (self-appointed) position, I judged her pretty enough to come to "my" house party. The girl liked to square dance as much as my girls did. She usually went to the pavilion with a boy named Frank, a husky, well-tanned fellow who looked sort of grumpy. All of them were Washingtonians, but I did not think I knew them until Sister told me the pretty girl's name was Flora and she was Mary Lee's cousin. Then I remembered. They were Billy's cousins, too, and I had been to their house once with Billy and met the boys. Flora and Frank were new, though.

I saw them that night at the pavilion, where the square dance was in full swing. Flora, like Sister and the girls, danced almost every set, both with visitors and islanders. That was what made Frank grumpy: he thought she should dance only with him. I heard all of these things later, for the events of that night were talked about a lot.

At the next break most everybody sat outside on the benches, but Frank steered Flora out to the end of the dock. A few minutes later Flora screamed "He jumped in! Help!" Somebody else yelled, "There's sharks out there." The crowd rushed to the end of the dock, Cap'n Bill, somehow in the lead. A lot of screaming and yelling started. One lady bellowed, "Sharks!" and fainted flat out on the dance floor.

Cap'n Bill took charge. He moved the crowd back to the pavilion. Lum Gaskill, the same man who had rescued Sister and Margaret and me the time we were drifting toward the inlet, took charge of Flora. She managed to sob that Frank tried to get her to promise not to dance with anyone else. When she refused to promise, Frank yelled, "I'll commit suicide, then!" and jumped.

The captain posted three Ocracokers with flashlights to look all around the dock, and he sent Jim Baugham and Owen to get a skiff. "Look under the dock," he instructed them. Friends hurried off to get Flora's and Frank's folks. The crowd calmed down, but the buzz of talk continued. The partner of the fainted lady picked her up and revived her by hugging and kissing her. She batted her eyes and moaned some.

After a little while, somebody on shore yelled "Here he comes!" and pointed to a figure walking up the shore. It was Frank, wearing a lop-sided grin, alive, though barnacle-scratched from hugging a piling. The boys in the skiff helped him up on the dock. Frank looked embarrased, but not for long. The fainted lady's partner released her and ran at Frank. "Scare everybody like that, will ye?" he hollered, and knocked Frank back over-board. The Gaskill boys fished him out again and that ended the night of the "dead" body at the Pamlico Inn. The talk about it went on for a long time, though.

I strolled out to the site of the "suicide" the next morning in time to hear Cap'n Bill and an older man talking about it. "Do you think the young fool intended to drown himself?" asked the old gentleman.

"Look here," the Cap'n answered, "What do you think?" He pointed to a pair of shoes with socks neatly rolled inside, parked beside a piling: Frank's shoes.

When I finally remembered to ask Sister if she thought Cap'n Bill knew about the secret showers, she laughed and said Cap'n Bill knew about everything that happened at the Inn.

"You know, Mac, when our crowd of girls and the other Washington people all attend the square dances, we're helping make the dances a success. Mr. Gaskill knows that. He tried to tell me he appreciated it, and we were welcome to use the Inn when we needed to. It was hard for Captain Bill to talk that way. He's better at telling people what to do." Sister said the girls knew how he felt. They just liked to pretend it was a secret oper-ation when they took a shower.

THE WRECK

I HAD SEEN THE WRECKAGE OF OLD SHIPS scattered along the beach, had heard accounts of shipwrecks from some of the islanders, and had been told about others by Lizzie and Bup. I read about wrecks in *Robinson Crusoe* and *The Swiss Family Robinson.* Bup commented that he thought the Robinson family had sailed in a department store instead of a ship, a remark I pondered until I understood what Bup meant.

I fantasized a shipwreck I would witness. It was to be a safe and sanitary shipwreck, with no lives lost. I imagined the ship, sails and rigging tattered and torn, driving through the breakers and crashing on the reef. Then I brought in the Coast Guard, with surf boats and Lyle guns. Some of the people were rescued by the surf boats, but the storm grew in fury until the Coast Guard had to rig the breeches buoy and rescue the rest of them. The last one to be rescued was the ship's captain, who rode in the breeches buoy holding the ship's dog in his arms. My imagination brought me back to the wreck the next day to find parts and pieces nicely distributed along the beach. I would salvage the steering wheel which would look good propped up against the wall of my room at home.

I waited a long time to see a shipwreck, but the one I finally encountered little resembled my imaginary one in size, scope, or location.

I started 'round the Creek one afternoon by the shore route and across the Goat Bridge. I spied a pretty little sloop, smaller than a skipjack oyster boat, entering the Creek. Her two-man crew hauled down the sails and started a putt-putt engine. The boat slowly approached the docks across the Creek. I began to trot so I could meet her and look her over and talk to the crew.

When I got to the Community Store's dock they had finished tying up the boat and were entering the store. I gave them a friendly hello and got a nod from one and a faint Hi from the other. I followed them to ask about their boat. One was named Tony, the other Rudy. They told Mr. Fulcher they were in school at Chapel Hill. They were older than me, about the age of Sister and the girls.

The black-haired one, Tony, was from Chicago and he owned the boat. He was a tall, thin young man with no chin. The cartilege saved in his chin construction had been used in a long pointed nose. With his long black sideburns, I thought he looked like a Canada goose. His companion was more muscular and had his blond hair cropped in what I called a German hair cut. He did not say where he came from, but he talked like Tony, only a little more.

The pair returned to their boat, and still I followed. They told me a little about the boat. She was twenty-four feet long, slept two uncomfortably in the little cabin, was round-bottomed, and had a centerboard. She also had a one cylinder Lathrop engine, the putt-putt I had heard. I remembered the big two-cylinder Lathrop, the engine from the *Lena Bell*, that Bup had stored in his barn.

They putted across the Creek and anchored along a vacant stretch of shore near the edge of the salt marsh. They pumped up a rubber dinghy for their landing (*I* would have *waded* ashore).

I sauntered toward home, intending to get a closer look at what they were up to. By the time I arrived at their campsite, they had pitched a pup tent and were making a camp fire. I wanted an invitation to go sailing, but did not want to ask directly, so I offered to help set up their camp. They declined my offer. Rudy did explain that they planned to cook on shore, but would sleep on the boat. He said they would rig a big bed in the cockpit and only use the cramped cabin in case of rain. They did not like to cook in that hot little cabin.

I hiked on home, feeling envious of the young men and covetous of their boat. There was a good chance that Tony and Rudy might show up at Bup's cottage if they could get somebody to introduce them and if they could pass Mama's inspection. I was pretty sure I would see them at Cap'n Bill's before long. I still wanted to sail in their boat.

I did not catch sight of them the next day, for I went 'round the Creek by the other route. What I did see, looking across the Creek from Mr. Big Ike's dock, was a gauzy looking tent rigged over the cockpit of the boat. Mr. Big Ike told me Tony and Rudy were at his store when he opened that morning and bought fifteen yards of mosquito netting. They had discovered who lived in the tall marsh grass!

Mosquito netting was used to cover most of the windows at Ocracoke. Daddy had explained to me that galvanized screen wire rusted out in one summer at the beach, and copper screening, which lasted much longer, was very expensive. Bup's cottage had copper screens in the hard-to-reach upstairs windows, but mostly it had cloth netting. The cloth stretched and sagged some, and in a flukey breeze it puffed in or puffed out. It looked like the house was breathing in on one side and out on the other.

I occasionally saw the boat out in the Sound and I glimpsed them once walking along the beach at dusk. Rudy had his arm around Tony as if Tony had been hurt someway, or was sick. They never came to the cottage or to the square dance. I thought how nice it would be to stroll by their camp with Sammy. He was about as old as those snotty sailors and twice as big. His size alone would get them to talk to us. In spite of his teasing, Sammy was nice to have around at times.

I hung around the pavilion more than usual that summer, even though Zoph was not playing. Mr. Jacobson was back leading the little band. I knew Mr. Jacobson at home where he had a band and also tuned pianos. When Mr. Jacobson's fiddle came alive it was as good as a whole orchestra. He played some songs I knew, like *Turkey in The Straw*. I mused that Mr. Jacobson and Zoph ought to go to Hollywood together.

I was sitting on the end of the bench nearest the door, about ready to leave, when a new boy walked in, looked all around, then spoke to me.

"Are you Mac?" he asked.

I jumped and gulped, "Yeah."

The stranger stuck out a big hand to shake and introduced himself as Johnny's cousin Joe. He was visiting the same uncle as Johnny for the first time, and Johnny had told him how to find me. Joe was a year older than I and considerably bigger, but our interests were the same. I thought when Joe grew up to his hands and feet he would be a giant. I promised to show him around.

I met him the next morning. We started 'round the Creek by the Goat Bridge so I could point out the sailor campers and their boat. "They're sort of sissy acting, but they sure got a nice boat."

Tony and Rudy were kindling a breakfast fire when we came up. They nodded to me, scrutinized Joe, and continued their preparations. We noticed the large folding knife Rudy was using to whittle kindling. It had a multitude of blades and gadgets folded into its bright red handle. Rudy, noticing our interest, told us it was a Swiss army knife, imported personally by his father from Switzerland. (Even the Swiss Family Robinson's department ship did not have such a knife!) Rudy crammed it back in his pocket without offering it for inspection.

We admired Tony's boat as we hiked past it. I saw the name *Dorian* painted on the stern and remarked, "What a dumb name. It sure ain't a dory. I know that much about boats. But I would like to go sailing in her." Joe agreed it was a dumb name but disagreed otherwise, "I don't much want to sail a boat with those two. But it sure is a nice boat."

I forgot about Tony and Rudy and *Dorian,* because a new guest came to the cottage who engaged my full interest. It was Uncle Whitey, Bup's oldest son and Mama's oldest brother. He had been to visit before, but this time I got to know him better.

Uncle Whitey was a Jr., named for Bup who had been named for a Confederate general, a friend of his father's. Bup used the name William Whiting McIlhenny; he was called Whiting when he was not called Mr. Mac or Bup, and thought those names were sufficient. Uncle Whitey thought it was a great joke being named for the old general, and within the family he called himself William Henry Chase Whiting McIlhenny. He joked sometimes that his third name was Chaste and sometimes it was Chased. Like Aunt Margaret, Uncle Whitey could enliven spirits and generate fun for all ages.

Whitey was above average height, broad-shouldered, and agile. He had the family's round face, but his was bisected by a trimmed mustache as black as his slicked-back hair. He was a stylish dresser, which I admired. Comparing Uncle Whitey to our one-time guest Monte, I decided Uncle Whitey was a genuine sport, because he knew a lot and did a lot, while Monte was an imitation who could only talk a lot to ladies.

Uncle Whitey was both attractive to and attracted by ladies. After Grandmother McIlhenny died, Mama and Aunt Margaret appointed themselves marriage counselors for their brothers. They were surprised and miffed when both selected wives without their big sisters' help, though they admitted that they were pleased with their choices. The two counselors then concentrated on selecting a husband for their baby sister, Mary Bell. That became a long campaign with little success.

Because Aunt Virginia did not accompany Uncle Whitey on this visit, Mama wondered if she needed to chaperone Uncle Whitey, but there was no need, he had come to visit family and old friends on the island, not ladies. Both Uncle Whitey and Uncle Harry had attended the Naval Academy. But while Uncle Harry was graduated and began his career in the navy, Uncle Whitey dropped out, on account of something about a professor's wife who was interested in Uncle Whitey more than was good for either of them. He resigned from Annapolis, continued his education in engineering, and became a civilian marine engineer. I never heard what happened to the professor's wife.

Uncle William Henry Chaste Whiting wanted to stroll around the island the next morning and meet old acquaintances. He invited me to come along. Mama nodded a hearty assent; I agreed at once. Uncle Whitey, like me, had spent many boyhood summers on the island and knew almost everybody we met. We passed Joe, on an errand for his aunt, and I introduced him to Uncle Whitey. I reserved the right to brag about Uncle Whitey later. Our conversations with Ocracokers were interspersed with my questions and Uncle Whitey's explanations of ships and shipyards. On the way back to the cottage Uncle Whitey talked to Mr. Styron about a ride to the beach that afternoon. The girls all wanted to go, as I did. Mama thought the responsibility of six late-teen girls and one brat would fully occupy Uncle Whitey's afternoon!

The girls adorned themselves in their best bathing suits, robes, towels, sandals, and big hats. I put on my scratchy old bathing suit and flung a towel over my shoulders. Uncle Whitey appeared in a dashing bathing suit, the finest I had ever seen. It was modest, but different (and it was not red). He wore short navy blue trunks held up by a white web belt with a shiny brass buckle. His sleeveless top was striped in blue and white horizontal bars with an emblem on the chest. The emblem was a dead rat, his feet in the air and his eyes shut.

Everybody admired the suit and questioned the emblem. Uncle Whitey sort of explained it, saying he belonged to a swimming club in Richmond and the rat was the club's insignia. "The Dead Rat Club?" I wondered. I examined the suit later when it hung on the clothesline. It was soft and smooth, not thick, itchy wool. I figured out the jockey strap inside and decided my next bathing suit would be one like that. When Sammy saw Uncle Whitey's suit, he had to have one right away. Mama asked Whitey to send him one, dead rat and all. Despite the temptation, I still preferred to swim in my everyday short pants or in nothing at all when I could.

The trip to the ocean was fine, the surf was high and we all rode the waves. Uncle Whitey swam like a porpoise. That night everybody went to the square dance. I stayed only a little while, for Uncle Whitey had brought me a parcel of books from Daddy and Lizzie.

Next morning I went to the Inn with Uncle Whitey. Cap'n Bill sat by us in the pavilion and talked to Uncle Whitey about ships and fish and old times on the island. I pointed out Tony and Rudy's sloop sailing in the Sound. Uncle Whitey called her a trim little craft. Cap'n Bill commented that she was too good for the pair to handle. He said Tony and Rudy, who sometimes ate supper in Miss Annie's dining room, had learned he had been a ship captain. They then asked him for sailing directions to Portsmouth Island.

"I told 'em to be damn careful sailing in that inlet." Turning to Uncle Whitey, he continued, "You know how treacherous it is out there, Whiting. I told 'em to stay in the marked channel and to mind the chart. There's water too shallow for even their little boat. Specially over towards Beacon Island. Hardly a foot of water on those shoals. I orter know. I was wrecked there meself in the 1899 blow."

That was the only time I heard Cap'n Bill mention his personal shipwreck, although I had heard about it. I guessed ship captains did not like to talk about their own shipwrecks. Anyhow, Cap'n Bill had just set a record for the longest conversation that I ever heard him make.

"Come to see me again, Whiting." The Cap'n wheeled around and hurried off, elbows pumping, tending to business once more.

Uncle Whitey embarked on the Washington boat early the next morning and the house party settled back into its normal routine. The house seemed dull. I broke away after "sam'witch" time, and met Joe, whereupon we decided to hike to Pointer Beach by the Sound shore. I was bragging some about Uncle Whitey, but changed the course of my conversation to tell Joe about discovering the rare Buffalo Toad during that long-ago summer. We continued past Springer's Point, wading along the marshy places and walking on the sandy beaches.

Black clouds hurried across the Sound. Gusts of wind ruffled the marsh grass and brought rain showers. We turned back for home. Tony's sloop was flying ahead of the storm, trying to beat it back to Ocracoke. The wind and rain increased, but we did not hurry, for a little wind and rain did not bother us overmuch. We were between Teach's Hole and Springer's Point when the line squall hit. The wind flattened the marsh grass and the rain lashed us in nearly horizontal sheets. We sheltered behind a cluster of cedar trees.

Through a break in the rain we glimpsed the sloop . She was close to the island, sails reefed, and in trouble. She seemed to be stuck fast, heeling way over toward shore. The jib blew loose, flew part way up the mast, and streamed like a flag. Tony and Rudy were scrambling around the cockpit trying to lift something. The boat began to move again, forward and sideways. Rudy climbed over the cabin to haul in the jib while Tony steered.

Rain obscured the view as the sloop washed sideways toward shore. We heard a crack, even above the wind's howling, and the boat capsized. She swung around, her rigging caught on something, one side awash. We saw Rudy clinging to the bow, his mouth opening, but we could not hear him yell. We did not see Tony. The boat was not a long way from shore.

Joe yelled, "We better go get 'em." I nodded. We waded into the heaving Sound. The water was some above our knees between waves but neck deep when a big sea rolled in. We pushed against the wind and waves; it was like swimming in a rough ocean, except for the rain. As we struggled closer to the wreck, the water's average depth was not over our heads, but big waves swamped us. It became difficult staying on our feet.

We heard Rudy, still hugging the boat's bow, yelling "Help! Help!" Then we saw Tony. He had one arm around the mast, with only his head above water, and it was bloody. Joe got to Tony first, untangled him from the sail and ropes, and started dragging him ashore. Tony was conscious, but acting goofy. I waded to Rudy, who was still hollering for help. I was concerned about how to carry Rudy, who was bigger and heavier than me. The problem solved itself when I slapped Rudy on the shoulder and yelled, "Put your feet down." Rudy looked astonished when he touched bottom. I had to guide him, but Rudy could walk.

When we deposited the survivors on the shore, the rain slacked off. Joe and I sat down to pant awhile and Tony and Rudy threw up together. All four of us sat in a line to rest. The wind dropped and the waves gradually decreased. The squall was past, the sloop *Dorian* was a mess. She lay on her side, her mast broken off at the deck, tethered by the halyards and stays. Floorboards, cushions, a piece of the center board, all the loose parts, were washing ashore. We asked Tony and Rudy if they could get up, but got no answer; both were still groggy. Tony's head looked raw, but was not bleeding any more. Rudy appeared unhurt. After a while Rudy groaned upright and tried to help Tony up. It took all three of us to get Tony on his feet. He finally managed a slow trudge down the shore. We told the two survivors we would help salvage the boat later, but got no answer.

Cap'n Bill had seen the sloop capsize, and sent two of his nephews in his truck to Mr. Springer's to check on the sailors. The Gaskill men met us on the beach and helped Tony and Rudy on the truck. Joe and I rode back to the Inn and got off. Cap'n Bill and Miss Annie sent the truck on to Miss Bragg's to get Tony's head repaired.

We went home for dry clothes and to tell our version of the afternoon. As I was relating events, it dawned on me that I had at last seen a shipwreck. This one had no Lyle gun, no breeches buoy, but it was still a shipwreck, or at least a boat wreck. There was no steering wheel to hang on the wall. The Coast Guard, however, did attend, though I was not there.

That evening the Chief of the station sent a crew in a picket boat to pull the wrecked sloop off the shore and into the Creek. As soon as Joe heard it, he hurried around to get me. We trotted to the Coast Guard Station to see "our" wreck, deck awash, with the broken mast and sails spread on the shore. We walked over for a closer look, when Tony, helped by Rudy, hobbled onto the dock. Tony was wearing a big, white turban Miss Bragg had constructed. Rudy told us that he and Tony were staying at the Pamlico Inn until Tony felt better and they had the boat repaired.

The Chief, holding a wallet stuffed with soggy bills, asked which one was Tony Whateverthisnameis? Tony answered and had manners enough to thank him. The Chief said they found only one wallet inside the cabin. Rudy said he did not have one. Tony asked the Chief if the Coast Guard would repair his boat. The Chief said no and added, "We'll bring ye in, but we don't repair wrecks." Then the Chief asked what happened to them.

When they saw the squall coming, Rudy told him, they decided to sail straight for the Creek and not follow the channel markers. The Chief grunted. The water looked all right, Rudy explained, but they hit something that jammed the centerboard sideways. They bumped free once, but struck again closer to shore, until the board broke off. That was about the time the jib tore loose. They washed sideways until they hit something that smashed the side and capsized them. Rudy was not sure what happened next, until he sort of came to, sitting on shore.

The Chief answered, "Them two brought ye ashore is what happened," and pointed to Joe and me. We were pleasantly embarrassed at this but I stopped myself from saying anything. Tony and Rudy seemed surprised. Two of the Coast Guardsmen towed the Dorian to a sandy stretch of beach near the head of the Creek. They helped Rudy bail her out. Tony helped bail some, but he was mostly a wounded survivor. Some of the island men brought wood rollers and they all helped tug the sloop out of the water. They told Tony and Rudy to drain the seawater from the engine right away.

Tony and Rudy had no idea what to do next and had to ask for more advice. I was tired of Tony and Rudy, but as I started to leave a discussion began among the Ocracokers about who was the best man to repair a round bilge boat. Some more islanders joined the talk. I sat back down to listen.

One man said get Thomas O'Neal, but another one said he was across the Sound—go find Mr. Scarborough. Old man Washington Creef over to Manteo was the best shad boat builder, another voice said. "That he was," commented still another, "but he's been dead forty year." "Well, his boys then," said the first, "or the Dough family to Manteo." Captain Dave's brother said a man named Guilford at Stumpy Point built round-hulled power boats. Tony and Rudy still did not know what to do, until Mr. Big Ike rumbled in. "One of ye go get Thomas O'Neal. He's back." Pointing to Tony and Rudy he added, "Thomas is your man."

Some of the Ocracokers drifted off, and Joe had to go home, but I stayed. Nothing could have induced me to leave all the boat-building talk. Mr. O'Neal arrived, probed and scraped the broken ribs and plank with his pocket knife, and allowed he could fix the damage. "These here are steam-bent frames. I cain't do them, but I've got some live oak sections I can cut natural-curve ribs from, and screw a batten over that broken strake. No mast timber, though. I can build ye a new centerboard." Tony asked if he could do it all right away. "No", answered Mr. O'Neal, "I can finish it by September if we all ain't washed away by then. And ye'll have to bring in a new mast. Farrow in Washington can get ye a spar if ye go back that way, and Dave or Ike can bring it here for ye. I'll help ye step it and rig it when you come back. Best I can do."

As I hurried back to the cottage (it was past supper-time), I ruminated about Tony and Rudy. Joe was right, I concluded, and I no longer wanted to go sailing with them either (although I had not been invited to go). They were not exactly highland terrapins, because they knew how to sail a boat—most of the time, anyhow. But they were out of place at Ocracoke. I sensed something different about Tony and Rudy, something I did not understand. It was not their being Yankees, because I knew some nice Yankees. I just did not like Tony and Rudy.

Joe and I were headed 'round the Creek the next morning, on some routinely urgent matter, taking the goat-bridge route, when we found Tony and Rudy at their camp site striking the tent and packing their gear. They had a skiff full of baggage and boat parts. Rudy said they had been told to store anything they wanted to leave in the cabin of the sloop, where it would be safe until they came back. He looked doubtful, but said that was what they would have to do. Tony wore a flat gauze patch taped to his head instead of his turban. He was pale and his sideburns were longer and blacker than ever. He looked even more like a goose. His nose seemed to have grown some.

They started to stammer something about the boat wreck, the first time they had mentioned it to us. They looked like they had just swallowed some of Aunt Lizzie's quinine. Rudy took over, but they sounded rehearsed.

"You saved our lives. We didn't know what happened at first. Unh."

Tony honked in with something like, "Uh, ah, gratitude- uh-thanks."

They took deep breaths, mumbled some more and stammered, "How can we, unh, ever repay you? Uh, anything at all?"

I was about to mumble an aw shucks kind of answer, when Joe spoke up. He was both quicker and sharper.

"Yeah," Joe answered, "you could give us that Swiss army knife to remember you by."

The visitors were apalled. "No, no!" Rudy gasped. "That's my most precious possession."

Tony backed him up, "No, not that! Think of something else."

Joe and I left the pair and their precious possession and continued 'round the Creek. We never saw Tony or Rudy again. Though we had nothing in remembrance of them, I never forgot them.

EXPLORATIONS
& EXPEDITIONS

OUR ADVENTURES WERE VARIED—sometimes contrived, often unplanned. I do not remember where we got some of our ideas.

Aunt Lizzie once read us a story about the Trojan War and a poem about one of the Greeks: Mr. Tennyson explained about Ulysses and his adventures.

> Much have I seen and known; cities of men
> And manners, climates, councils, governments
> Myself not least, but honor'd of them all;
>> And drunk delight of battle with my peers,
> Far on the ringing plains of windy Troy.
> I am a part of all that I have met.

It was not like that with us. We had not been anywhere very distant, done anything great, nor even seen much. We had heard about a lot of things, read about events, and had seen the Saturday afternoon continued pictures, so I guess those things could have been a part of us. I doubt if Ulysses read anything and I know he did not go to the movies, so we knew some things he did not. If he had been to Troy, I had been to Raleigh.

We met a lot of strange people and climes at the Reita Theater in the Saturday afternoon movies. Ulysses met the Cyclops, giants, and the Sirens, while we met fierce Indians and cannibals. He saw the great Achilles, but we met Zungu in the jungles of the Reita.

We liked the jungle serials better than Cowboy and Indian pictures or war stories. The different serials, all similar in format, portrayed a young couple who were explorers or scientists travelling the jungles of Africa or South America with native bearers on Safari (that was the way we wanted to explore Ocracoke) and were naive enough to trust the villains. The chief jungle villain was a white man who wore a dirty white suit and promised the heroes he would take care of everything for them. They always believed him.

The one I remember best continually misled the young couple by saying, "I, George E. Cuttelass am your fran'." Then he delivered them to the natives, and Zungu stepped in. The dark-skinned natives tended to eat their prisoners or sacrifice them to the gods. Zungu, a low budget Tarzan, usually managed to rescue the innocents. One variation had Zungu captured by the cannibals and tied to a stake. The tribesmen surrounded him and chanted their victory song to the beat of the tom-toms. The Hollywood script writers did not work very hard on that chant: "No mo Zungu" *tom tom tom* "No mo Zungu" *tom tom tom*. After the first showing of this masterpiece, the front rows of movie fans joined with vigor in "No mo Zungu," which always brought Aubrey, the manager, down front to flap his hands and shut us up.

We were part of all that we had read, heard, and seen on the screen.

Old Ulysses might have seen more places than we had, but we knew all about the river (or thought we did), from its butt joint confluence with the Tar all the way down to the Sound and across to Ocracoke. Only the mysterious interior of the island eluded us.

As soon as I began to learn the geography of the island, I became intrigued by the section called Up Trent. I did not know exactly where it was and the answers to my questions were too vague to tell me. I had been to Pointer Beach and I knew where Down Below was, but Up Trent beckoned. During Lee's second summer at Ocracoke we began serious planning for an expedition to camp out and explore the place. I was ten years old, Lee eleven, men of experience.

We started to list the equipment needed. It was to be a first-class safari, like the ones in the Saturday movies. I knew where we could get a tent, and Lee had two canteens and a compass. We would have to cook, so we wrote down a frying pan and some tin plates and cups. We added a coffee pot as standard equipment, although neither of us drank coffee. Lee told about visiting a cave some boys had dug in Wanoca and drinking tea out of scallop shells for cups. That was neat, he said. We listed a tea kettle, too. We planned on finding the shells Up Trent. Explorers always sat around the camp fire at night, so we added some folding camp chairs.

Next we began listing the food we would have to carry. The first item on the list was peanut butter. We could not decide between crackers and light bread, so wrote down both. Bread led to jam, then cheese, then baloney, then mustard. Some sardines and some "hyena" sausage made nice variations. We listed salt and pepper, coffee and tea, and sugar. We thought we could catch fish to fry and we planned on eating sea gull eggs (both of us remembered how hard it was to transport eggs unscrambled). Fried fish called for corn bread, so we added a sack of corn meal and a sack of flour. Various other items came to mind—we added grease, fish hooks and line, a spatula, blankets, a clock, a gig and a dip net. We sat back, satisfied with our planning, and reviewed the lists.

The more we studied all those composition book pages, the bigger the imaginary pile of equipment grew. We could never carry it all, we needed help. Bearers and a safari were the answer, and the key man was Julius. We would have to approach him very carefully. He might not like being head bearer; even if he wanted to go, he might want to be head man and leader. Chief scout sounded much better than head bearer, we decided. We caught up with Julius that very evening as he started home. His house was in a thick grove in the middle of the island, nearly on the edge of the ocean beach. We walked with him, stammered false starts, and finally lurched into a sort of invitation.

"We thought maybe you might want to go camping with us. We're gettin some camp stuff together," I started.

Lee added, "We want to explore Up Trent."

Julius knocked the plan in the head right away. "Campin'? Me and Mr. Gary too busy for any campin'. Whut for ye want to go up Trent? Ain't nuthin' much there. First day Mr. Gary give me some time off, I kin show ye the way. Best way's on a truck. Mr. Ike got a farm up thatta way, ye could ask him to take ye sometime. We got plenty fishin' parties and when we ain't, Miss Lena always got things to do. Campin'—haw!"

I asked Doss if Julius had any brothers and she informed me that he did and they were both gone to sea. That ended the plan for the safari, but the exploration plan was only postponed.

The Up Trent exploration finally took place the next year—I think it was 1935. It began on a dull, itchy kind of day—nobody new in the house and the girls busy with clothes and hair and other dull things. Nobody interesting was at Cap'n Bill's or on the beach. I sat on the front steps and gaped at nothing.

Johnny came loping up the road, halted, and clawed at the sky in the mud fiddler style salute we used with each other. He had a boat to use the next day, for all day, he told me. His uncle had loaned his skiff, the smaller one. Johnny told me to be ready early and to bring something to eat and some drinking water; then he executed an impressive departure. The entire complexion of the day changed.

The girls were all upstairs, Mama was lying down, so I thought the time was right for my preparations. I began by building a stack of my currently favorite sandwiches—baloney and cheese with mayonnaise, the layers mortared fast with peanut butter—then hid my lunch bag in a corner of the icebox. I found an empty jug which I rinsed and filled at Mr. Bragg's outdoor pump. The water tasted faintly of vinegar. "Good," I thought, "prevents scurvy." I stored the jug under the side porch.

That night at supper I casually mentioned that Johnny's uncle would let us use his skiff, and that we wanted to row past the Coast Guard station and up the little creek on the other side. Mention of the Coast Guard Station was supposed to sound reassuring. Mama approved the plan, with the caution not to go out in the Sound, to stay close to shore, and to be careful, the usual maternal sailing directions.

I gobbled an early breakfast of shredded wheat and evaporated milk. Mama looked out her door and repeated her sailing directions. I assented with perfect sincerity, as our objective was land exploring, not seafaring. I retrieved my lunch bag, extracted the water jug, and trotted down the path to meet my co-captain.

We found the skiff tied to a little pier, boarded, and "sitting well in order, smote the sounding furrows." The heavy skiff handled very well, with each of us pulling an oar as we left the Creek and rounded the Coast Guard station. We gazed at the cutter moored to the dock and at the surf boats under the shed. Johnny's kin, unlike many island families, had no members in the Coast Guard, so we had no entree there. We both thought the base was, somehow, top secret.

Johnny's uncle had given him sailing directions, and a geography lesson. We entered a little bay that Johnny said was called Mary Ann's Pond, even though it was not really a pond, with land all around it. The gentle wind was from dead astern and we found that one of us could manage both oars. We poled the skiff where the water was shallow and the bottom sandy. Past another point we entered another bay called North Pond. This one had a pier with a sunken skiff by it. We landed where a little path lured us inland to explore the territory. Back from the shore was a closed-up house. This one, unlike Mr. Springer's, which was tall and gray, sat low, spread-out, brown, and equally vacant. We were not much interested in houses; we wanted to find hills and jungles and new country. Back to the boat we went.

North Pond-Bay was big, but we finally rounded Horsepen Point (though we saw neither pen nor horses). The shore changed direction and character, becoming marshy with lots of seaweed and spike rushes. We each swigged from the anti-scorbutic water jug. The water was warm, so we covered the jug with wet seaweed. The marsh seemed miles long, but finally we discovered a beach of golden sand where the sand dunes and live oak trees grew almost to the water's edge. We beached the boat, swim-tested the water, and began serious exploring.

We discovered tree-clad dunes, but no houses. There were Bullis grape vines, though the grapes were not yet ripe. I suggested we call this country Vinland, a suburb of Up Trent. Johnny agreed and declared that it was dinnertime, so we raced back to the boat. A small, bleached, wood grating washed up in the sand served as a table. We pooled my sandwiches and his ham biscuits and baked sweet potatoes along with the scurvy-preventing water. The two Vikings fell to feasting and ate every crumb. Then, appetites sated, bellies bloated, we stretched out in the sand, talked awhile, then slept. We awoke to a westering sun and a hard wind with noisy waves. After a quick swim, we shoved off for home.

The return voyage was so different. For one thing, the wind was dead-foul. The heavy skiff fought her way, her flat bottom lifting over one wave and pounding down on the next one and every oar stroke was an effort. The marshy shore that had seemed long was now endless. We sweated and pounded away, inching toward home. We reached Horsepen Point in darkness, resting in the next bay as we drank the last of the water. We were not lost, for we could see the light house winking at us from a million miles ahead. We crept and pounded along, not talking much any more. The glow of lights at the Coast Guard Station appeared at last. We rowed, slower and slower, past the Station and into the Creek.

Johnny's uncle was waiting at the pier. He spoke sharply to Johnny about the time—past ten o'clock, he said. To me he said only, "Go home. Your mother's worried." Johnny asked his uncle if we could wait until morning to clean up the skiff. He answered only, "Go home. Both of ye."

I dragged to the cottage, tireder than I could remember ever being, and hungrier and thirster than I ever wanted to be again. The lamps were bright in the house, Mr. Bragg and Julius met me on the front porch, surprising me. "He's here," Mr. Bragg called back in the house, then he and Julius clumped off.

Mama rushed out, Sister trailing her. She hugged me hard and wailed, "We thought you were drowned." Then she grasped my shoulders and shook me so hard my teeth rattled. Sister tried to restrain her, so Mama released her hold. They both led me into the house. I was astonished, on top of worn out, at Mama's behavior. I wondered, "Why were they so wrought-up?"

Mama got mad. "You scared us to death. Whatever is the matter with you coming home this late? We were about to send for the Coast Guard, when Gary Bragg said he would take his boat to look for you. You've alarmed the whole island. Haven't you got any sense at all?" And so on.

I thought, "*You've* alarmed the whole island, not me," but I had enough sense not to say it.

Still struck dumb, I sat down at the table. Mama, calmer, asked if I were hungry. I mumbled, "Yes'm and thirsty, too."

Sister brought me a big glass of ice water. I drank half of it, laid my head on my arm, and slept where I sat. I did not remember going to bed.

Next morning Mama served me an extra big breakfast. She told me to go on out, but she would talk to me later about my inconsiderate behavior. She further instructed me to apologize to Mr. Bragg for causing so much trouble. I considered that, but felt dubious about approaching Mr. Bragg in case he was as mad as Mama. I decided I would do it through Julius.

When I found him later that day, Julius told me Mama had sent the girls out to ask people if they had seen us. Julius said that when he and Mr. Bragg heard where we had gone they knew why we were late coming home. They were going to search for us to ease Mama's worries. From the immeasurable heights of his superior age and experience, Julius advised me, "You sho' got a lot to learn about boats and wimmen."

I walked down to the shore and crawled into my thinking place under Mr. Bragg's pier. I tried to understand how Mama could be worried, glad, and mad all at the same time.

MEAL TEA

DESPITE JULIUS' ADVICE TO ME, I thought I knew a lot in those days; it was easy for me to become an expert. I quickly learned to swim with an overhand stroke, and rejected the dog-paddle as babyish. If anybody had suggested we swim to Portsmouth, I would have started. As soon as I learned to row a skiff, I was an expert on small-craft. I did retain enough gumption not to flaunt my expertise before Daddy or Bup or Captain Ike—or Aunt Lizzie. Two subjects defied me, however. One was girls and why they behaved the way they did. The other was the things old people drank, all the different kinds of things.

The first kind of strong drink I heard about was whiskey—I had drunk a spoonful of it that time time I had the toothache. The time we visited the Portagee schooner, people were talking about rum-running. (Why running?) We had preserved the Buffalo Toad in what the island men called corn likker, the stuff with the smell that stabbed your nose. Other names I heard were booze, gin, rye, and tonic. One of the Pantegonians secretly bragged that he had some Scotch. All those names were confusing. Nobody answered the questions I asked, but instead told me I did not need to know.

Now, there was this new stuff, "meal tea," that the girls giggled about with some of the younger Ocracokers if Mama was not around. I decided I had better investigate this meal tea.

The place to start seemed to be the dance pavilion. There were many good dancers, the house-party girls agreed, but Mr. Big Ike was the very best. Most named Sam Creech near the top, but said it was best to dance with Mr. Creech early in the evening. They all laughed in agreement. I asked Sister why. She answered that, if he sweated much during the dance, he smelled like meal tea. Sam Creech was the key to meal tea, I decided.

I watched Mr. Creech the following night and followed him when he went out on the dock at the next intermission. I sat down on a bench near him, but all I could smell was hair tonic. One of the Ocracokers asked Sam Creech if he was ready for a little something. They walked out to the end of the dock by the big oil tank. I trailed them, trying to act casual with my tuneless whistling. Three men stood there, mumbling, and I saw one pass a quart jar around, so I eased closer. One of the Ocracokers stared at me, then spoke," You're Mac? You better go back to the dance hall." I wheeled around, back to the bench. After a few minutes they all trooped along the dock and entered the pavilion. The man who had spoken to me grinned and winked as he passed. The music restarted inside. Alone on the dock, I scooted out to the end to search all around the oil tank and piping and behind the crates and stuff. I found nothing, not even an empty jar. What had they done with it? I returned to the pavilion.

After several more dances, I watched Sam Creech mop his face with his handkerchief as he escorted a lady to her seat. He headed out the door, his wet shirt stuck to his back. I sidled after him and found a seat just downwind. This time there was more than hair tonic to smell. Mr. Creech was sour. Not like sour pickles, but something hard to describe. The aroma reminded me of a bowl of oatmeal somebody had left on the back porch all day, with maybe a little nose-zinging frog preserver added. It was not a nice smell; I understood what the girls meant. That was all I learned about meal tea that summer.

Many years later Elizabeth O'Neal Howard taught me how to make meal tea. She had never made any herself, she said, but she learned about it when she worked in her father's store. "If some of the boys [she meant young men] came in and bought a lard stand, five pounds of sugar, five pounds of corn meal, and a yeast cake, you knew what they were doing. They would stir it all up with water, punch a little hole in the lid and let it work. If they could wait, they got meal tea."

Elizabeth told me about one friend of hers who bought the ingredients. She tried to discourage him by telling him how harmful the stuff was. He challenged her to tell him anything bad that meal tea would do to him. "I couldn't think of anything else, so I told him it would give him Trench-Mouth. He laughed at me, and for the rest of his life he greeted me with, 'Haven't got Trench-Mouth yet.'"

My friend Owen of Ocracoke had made and sampled meal tea. His formula was similar. "You throw in a few dried apples or apricots for flavor. After it works, it'll knock you on y'r ass. It's kind of grainy unless you strain it good." When I asked him what it tasted like he said "Sort of like beer, but different."

John Irvin, a neighbor who spent summers at Hatteras all through his high school years, said the Hatterasers made it too. On his part of the island, though, there were a lot of mulberry trees, he told me, so the favorite home brew was mulberry wine in a lard stand. "It would have been right good if they had ever let it finish working, but they drank it up early." I imagine it was the same with meal tea. I still have not sampled meal tea.

BUP

ONE MARCH DAY, warm and spring-like, Mama met me at the front door on my return from school. "Go straight down to the store. Your father wants to talk to you." She was smiling, so I knew I was not in any kind of trouble, but I was puzzled. I took my short cut through the alleys which was not really much longer than following the sidewalk.

Daddy was in the office and he smiled, too. "Sit over there, Son," he said and pointed to the customer's chair beside his big stand up desk. "We've heard you talk about boats for a long time now. Your Grandfather and I think you're old enough to have your own skiff. We hope you've got enough sense to be careful with it. Mr. Mac [what Daddy called Bup] is going to build it and I will furnish the material. It's a birthday present from all of us.

"You'll have to do two things yourself. You're going to help Mr. Mac build it and learn all you can about boatbuilding. That's the first thing. The second thing is you'll listen to both of us when we tell you about safety and seamanship. We do not want you to be a highland terrapin." Daddy reached out to give my hair an affectionate ruffle.

Almost speechless, I managed to gulp, "Yeah—sure—yessir."

Daddy spoke again, "Then go around to Mr. Mac's and see what the schedule is. He's expecting you."

I neither walked nor ran to Bup's house—I soared. I lit panting in Bup's backyard where the old man was sharpening his handsaws. "Daddy said you'd—we'd—a boat—build a boat." I stammered the words almost too fast to understand.

Bup always proceeded at his own pace, so he sat me down on a sawhorse. "We've got some planning to do, some people to see, and some things to buy," Bup told me. "If you come around here Saturday morning, we'll get started. Come at 7:30 and I'll fix us some breakfast."

"Sure," I agreed. I would have agreed to anything Bup said. Besides, I liked Bup's pancakes, which were the same size as the bottom of the skillet. It did not take many to fill you up.

"The first thing we need to do is to talk to Andrew Emory about the boat and look at some of his. Your father is furnishing the material, but we'll select it. Be here Saturday."

On Saturday morning, well-ballasted with Bup's flapjacks, I followed him across the street and down the block to Mr. Emory's boatwright shop. I liked walking with Bup to the docks. Bup had been a cotton factor before he retired and had spent a lot of time at the docks shipping cotton. He knew everybody there. The biggest, blackest colored man I had ever seen came around a shed, stopped, and smiled at us. "Hello, Mr. Mac," the big man said. "Where's yo' cloak?"

"Good mornin', Gordon. Too warm for it." Bup answered. They both burst into laughter. "How is your wife now, Gordon?" Bup added.

"She a lot better, thank you for askin'. See you."

I was puzzled by the exchange. I knew Bup sometimes wore a long boat cloak in cold weather. It was something one of Bup's sons in the navy had sent him. Bup noticed my look and explained. Gordon had a slow-witted nephew that he brought to work when Bup needed extra help, for he worked hard under

Gordon's supervision. One cold, rainy day the nephew saw Bup in the boat cloak, the high collar turned up, the long, voluminous cloak hanging to his ankles. "Mr. Mac, is you a nun?" he asked. It was Bup and Gordon's private joke.

Grandpa and I passed two big gas boats under construction and entered Mr. Emory's shavings-littered, good smelling shop. Mr. Emory knew what we wanted and was glad to help. He showed us an unfinished skiff, upside-down on trestles. "This is a full sixteen-footer. Probably bigger than you want." He led us outside and pointed to a smaller boat tied to his dock. "That one's just over fourteen and a half feet, built of sixteen-foot stock."

"Yes," said Bup. "What do you think, Mac?"

"Yessir!" came my instant response. I was ready to agree with anything Bup said.

Mr. Emory and Bup talked some more about measurements and kinds of lumber. Bup thanked Mr. Emory, and I echoed him. As we left, Mr. Emory called after us, "Son, come back if I can help you." I observed that Mr. Emory sure was a nice man. Bup agreed and added, "Damn best boat builder I ever knew. When he puts wood together, it looks like it grew that way."

We headed for the saw mill. Bup's friend Mr. Anson recommended some good curly-grain cypress just out of the dry kiln. "Andrew Emory ordered some of it yesterday," he said.

Bup picked out several wide boards, telling me two of them were for the sides. Next Mr. Anson showed us the juniper stack of narrower planks that Bup wanted for the bottom. Bup ordered some of that, and a thicker piece of heart pine. Mr. Anson promised to deliver it Monday morning.

"One more stop, Mac," Bup told me as we entered the cabinet shop. Mr. Snuggs, a big fat man, was to shape the stem of the boat. Bup said that would save him a lot of hand labor. Mr. Snuggs rummaged through a stack of short lumber and handed me a two-foot billet so heavy I almost dropped it. The billet smelled like turpentine. Just then the mill's steam whistle went off so loud that I jumped and did drop it. Embarrassed, I snatched it up and handed it back to Mr. Snuggs. "Twelve o'clock," Bup announced, "Time to go home." Mr. Snuggs promised to shape the stem first-thing Monday.

As soon as we entered Bup's workshop I asked him when the boat would be finished. "A long time yet," Bup answered. "We can get set up for work this afternoon so we'll be ready to start building Monday or Tuesday afternoon when we have the lumber." I suggested I could skip school on Monday. "Absolutely not," Bup snapped. "Don't start that kind of craziness, or the work stops."

The rest of the afternoon and Monday were spent setting up two saw horses under the pecan tree in front of the workshop. We leveled and braced the sawhorses, then collected some old boards from under the shop. I questioned the use of second-hand boards, so Bup answered "We'll use these for moulds and frames and templates. You'll see what they are."

Tuesday was better—the mill had sent the lumber, piles of it were lying in Bup's garage. Grandpa and I picked the prettiest two of the wide boards and placed them on the sawhorses. Bup explained that the mill had sawed some of the wide boards into narrower strips for him. "Saves me lots of hand saw ripping."

Here I first learned there were no square corners on a boat, and few straight lines. Bup marked a slanted line on each end of one board and sawed along it. "Gives her some rake on bow and stern." I thought about getting a notebook to write down new words. "Now we'll give her some tuck-up at the stern." He clamped and tacked a narrow strip along the bottom edge of the board and bent it partway up at the stern. After walking all around it and looking at it from both ends, he handed me a pencil and told me to scribe a line along the strip, "A good heavy line." Bup removed the strip, hefted his narrow bladed saw and cut along the line. He smoothed with his plane, sighted along the curve, nodded, and said, "There. Let's move it." We placed the formed board on the uncut one and scribed the lines. Bup sawed and smoothed the second side. "Now we're ready to start putting her together."

We temporarily nailed two of the pre-cut strips along the bottom edge of the side boards. Bup drilled and countersunk holes for screws and put me to driving the screws. "These pieces are called *chines*." Another word for the notebook. Bup handed me a bar of soap and explained how a little soap on the threads made screw-driving easier. "You can fasten a boat with copper nails, brass screws, or galvanized nails," he continued. "Your Daddy sent brass screws. They're best. You don't mix brass and galvanized under water. One eats up the other. Galvanic action, its called. We can use galvanized boat nails above water if we want to. Get the wide thick piece of timber off my work bench in yonder. We'll shape the transom today." That was a long speech for Bup, with more new words.

"*Transom?*" I asked, puzzled: I thought about the hinged glass panels over the doors at home.

"The stern—the stern. The stern board for the boat. Bring it here."

Bup cut more of the narrow boards into ribs which I screwed in place on the side boards. They stuck over the top some, as Bup explained a narrow strake would go on top. *Strake* went in the mental notebook. Bup nailed one of the second-hand boards on top of the front saw horse, and a longer board on the rear one. "Now," he said, "We'll take a big step. Fetch me the stem from the workbench."

I ran in for the heavy, turpentiney chunk. I had not noticed it before. It was now shaped like a double arrowhead, two feet long, and still smelled the same. Bup fitted and planed some more, called me to hold it in place, and screwed one side board to the stem. He set the side on its bottom edge, secured it with a batten, and, with me holding, screwed the other side to the stem.

The two sides and stem formed a wide vee, with the sides resting on the rear saw horse extenders. "Time to build the moulds. Andrew Emory's coming over to help us plan." We sat in the old porch swing tied to the other side of the pecan tree. Bup rolled a cigarette while we waited.

Mr. Emory and Bup talked, measured, and figured, and I listened. Bup sawed two pieces of the wide boards saying, "The moulds are frames to bend the sides around to give her the right shape. When we're finished with 'em, we'll use the pieces for the seats."

The next day was Saturday and I came early. Bup had finished the moulds by the time Mr. Emory and Gordon arrived. We tacked the shorter mould in place on one side board. Bup brought out a piece of rope while Mr. Emory and Gordon pressed the two open ends of the vee together. I tried to both help and stay out of the way, a tough job. When the two side boards closed on the mould, Bup tied his rope tight around the open ends, which were still far apart. He stuck a short billet of wood in the rope loop and began to twist it. The sides drew closer together. Gordon held the long mould in place until both sides pressed on it. Mr. Emory nailed it in place. Bup fastened his winder and said, "Thank you both, Andrew. I can handle it now."

"She looks good, Mr. Mac. I'll come back when you need me." To me he added, "I mought hire you later to build skiffs, if Mr. Mac gives you a good report." I did not know how to answer, so I just grinned. Grins came easy then.

Bup fixed another rope loop with a longer winding board that scraped the ground when he twisted it. I thought of the rig as a tourniquet until Bup said it was a *Spanish windlass* (another term for the notebook). Bup twisted slowly and carefully, the sides came closer together, forming a nice boat shape.

"Mac," he said, "You be ready with your hammer and some nails and that transom. We'll draw it in slow and easy. Want to be sure both sides bend evenly. Stay off to one side until I call you, then jump to it with the stern transom." He continued to wind, his eyes flicking from the two sides to the windlass. I straddled the end of the extender board of the rear sawhorse, now clear of the side board, and started to see-saw on it. The extender board broke with a resounding crack, dumping me on the ground. Bup jumped three feet in the air, swearing "Hell-fire!" on the way up and "Damnation!" coming down. The windlass flopped back a half-turn. Bup thought one of the sides had broken. A quick look around showed him intact sides and me sprawled on the ground, red with chagrin and mute for once.

Bup started to laugh with relief. He could not stop laughing. Finally he managed to speak to his prostrate helper. "Have I got a boat builder or a damned monkey helping me? Get up and hold the transom in place. Get some screws ready—the long ones. Get the hammer and the long iron screw-clamp." I hustled. "Let's fasten the stern before you wreck the ship." I hoped Bup would not tell anybody about the incident. We clamped and screwed the transom in place without further trouble. Bup just said, "Good job." Then he sat in the swing and rolled another of his Bull Durham cigarettes.

Mr. Emory and Big Gordon came again that evening. We all turned the boat bottom-up on the saw horses, almost ready for the bottom planking, the keel, and the skag. Bup sawed off the remaining extender plank ends. He leveled the bottom edge of the side boards with his plane, planed the matching bevel on the transom, and sawed off the extra length of the stem. Then we were ready.

Bup let me cut some of the bottom planks from the juniper boards. He marked them for me to saw beveled and slanted to fit the curve of the sides. Nothing was square. Most of what I cut fitted and Bup said we could use the wrong cut pieces some-where else. Next he put me to drilling and screwing the boards in place while he cut and fitted ahead. Bup stuck a strip of sheet iron between each plank as I fastened it, leaving the same-sized crack between all the boards. When I asked why we were leaving cracks Bup explained it left room for the boards to swell in the water without buckling. There was a lot to learn.

I learned to use a thing Bup called a rose-head countersink to cut a neat little crater for the screw heads to fit in. When the planking was all done we fastened a four-inch-wide plank along the center of the bottom, the keel, with a slot sawed out of its stern part. The bottom, following the curve sawed in the side boards, slanted toward the top edge of the boat. Bup fitted a plank to this curve and fastened it in the slot in the keel. The *skag*, he called it, was a sort of keel extension and a straight rudder.

Bup trimmed the ends of the bottom planks with his super-sharp plane, then started me to rasping and sandpapering the ends smooth. He brought out a pot and began mixing white lead, a can of putty, some pine tar, and a little melted bee's wax. His new pudding-putty was ready by the time I finished sanding. He showed me how to smooth it over the countersunk screw heads. "Don't leave such a big lump," Bup directed, "You'll have to sand it smooth later. Just be sure the cavities are full."

The bottom was finished.

Daddy, Mr. Emory and Big Gordon all came at the same time that evening. We turned the boat upright. Everybody admired her, and I was the foremost. I was already imagining rowing the finished skiff. The following day, Friday, I would be out of school on account of a teachers' meeting; I was looking forward to a great two days; and the following week would bring the end of school, so I hoped the boat would be finished before we left for Ocracoke in July. Aunt Lizzie and I no longer went to Ocracoke in June, because she was preparing to open a small kindergarten in the fall. Anyhow, the boat-building monkey went home well pleased with himself.

Bup cut and fitted the long tapered top strake. I helped him screw it in place, and Bup planed it into a pleasing curve on top. We added a reinforcing strip inside along the tops of the ribs and edge-bent a thinner strip that covered the edge of the top strake, the rib tops, and the inside strip. Bup called that piece the *gunnel*. (When I finally did remember to start my boat-word note book, I asked Bup how to spell gunnel. His answer surprised me: "g-u-n-w-a-l-e.")

Any time I was not actually helping Bup, I was sanding. I wore out a lot of sandpaper and cultivated a lot of blisters and callouses, but I was proud of them. We built the small fore deck, the big seat in the stern, the two cross-ways rowing seats, and various braces. We added a half-round rub-rail on the top strake just under the gunnel. Bup announced the building was almost complete, with painting and fitting-out only still to come.

The following day, while Bup was cleaning up our shipyard and I was finishing sandpapering, Daddy came around. He brought a paint brush, a can of turpentine and a bucket of paint. The label proclaimed it was Woolsey's Yacht and Deck Paint and had a picture on it of a great sea serpent. Daddy and Bup sat in the swing, I perched on the end of a sawhorse.

Daddy told me, "You paint her. We'll watch. Paint everything white for the first coat. You can pick trim colors and bottom paint later."

Bup added, "We need to seal the surface now before we fit her out, and allow plenty of time to dry." He then demonstrated to father and son how he could roll a cigarette using only one hand and his teeth. He succeeded, although I thought the result looked more like a pigtail. I did not say it because anything Bup did or said was fine with me.

I chose light green paint for the inside of the boat and for the rub-rail. The seats and outside were white and the bottom red. The painting part was slow, with much time spent waiting for a coat to dry and cleaning up dribbles of the wrong color, the messy result of haste. I had to call for help twice to turn the ship over to paint another part. I realized I could not finish before the

Ocracoke trip in July. With the pressure of rushing off me, I enjoyed the work more and worried Bup less.

I had one problem that nagged at me while I sanded and painted—what to name the boat. I considered naming her for Lizzie, for Mama, and for Sister; I thought of Wookie and Evelyn and Miriam, all my Ocracoke favorites; then there was Grace, the girl I liked best in school—I had told her about the boat. I chortled to myself at the thought of the boat with all those names painted on it, stretching from stem to transom.

I finally consulted Pa about it. He helped. "You do have a problem, son. I'll talk to your mother and Lizzie for you. They'll appreciate the thought and understand. I think I'm going to buy some land at North Creek, and I'll get a fishing skiff to keep there. We can name her for Sis—Mary M. would be a good boat name. As for the rest of the ladies on your string, you'll have to decide for yourself." (What does "on a string" mean, I wondered. Like fish?)

Daddy continued, "You don't have to have a girl's name for a boat. Why not name the boat for your grandfather. He built her for you and he would like it if you did." And that is what I did. If any nosey outsider or highland terrapin wanted to know what the name *Bup* meant, I would tell them it was Portuguese.

One mid-June afternoon I cruised into Bup's backyard and saw an unexpected but familiar object. It was the Ocracoke icebox. Bup looked up to say, "No boat work this afternoon, Mac. You can help me on this. Ice compartment was leaking. Gary Bragg sent the box. I've built a new bottom grid. White oak. The old juniper one broke when those big blocks of ice fell on it. Getting a new liner, too. Macon is making that." Bup was talking about Macon Cogdell who ran the tin shop for Pa. He was as noted a tinsmith as Andrew Emory was a boat builder.

I helped Bup finish the grid, then helped Macon when he brought the new, shiny zinc liner. I passed Macon the hot soldering irons from the charcoal pot while Macon was soldering in the drain pipe.

"Who brought the icebox, Bup?" I asked.

"Came up on the *Russell L.*," Bup told me. "She's hauled out at Bill Warner's getting her bottom painted."

As soon as Bup and Macon were through with me, I took off for Mr. Warner's shipyard to inspect the Ocracoke boat out of water.

Russell L. looked bigger up on the marine railway than she did in the water. She had a man's name, so it seemed funny to call her she, but that is the way with boats. Two men were scraping her bottom, getting ready to paint. Captain Ike and Mr. Warner were working near the propeller, and another man, Captain Ike's nephew, was re-bolting the rudder straps. I walked all around the boat inspecting, hoping somebody would ask me to help, but they did not know I was an experienced boat builder. I could see that the hull was pointed at both ends, just as Sammy had once told me. The square stern I had seen from the deck looked like a porch overhanging up top.

Bup came over in a little while to ask Captain Ike when he could take the icebox aboard. Mr. Warner said the ship would be back in the water by 9 o'clock; Cap'n Ike said he could load the box then. He said he had a little freight to load and a small shipment of lumber from the sawmill to put aboard. Dave Williams, in the *Preston*, he added, was coming up Friday for the regular weekend trip, and he would be back on schedule the next Wednesday. He wanted to sail as soon as he could the next morning.

I asked Bup how long rudder hinges would last. Bup answered, "A long time, but they're called rudder *hangers,* not hinges." Then he asked me if I still kept that notebook of boat building words. I answered yes, so Bup added, "Well, here're two nice ones for you: *gudgeon* and *pintle.*" I gulped and Bup laughed. "The pintle is the part with the sort of shaft on it—it's bolted to the rudder. The gudgeon has a socket on it that the pintle's shaft fits in. The gudgeon's bolted to the ship's stern post. The pair of 'em are the rudder hangers."

Bup and I headed home. As I walked to my own house I considered those new words. I would put them in the book and I would use them as my private words for something else. I liked them better than the names I had heard on the school grounds.

As I turned the corner to leave Water Street, an idea seized me. A plan germinated in my mind that was almost complete when I reached home. I could make an extra trip to Ocracoke by myself on account of an unusual situation at home. Daddy and Mama were leaving early the next morning to spend a few days with Uncle George in Virginia. Mr. Walker would run the store and Sammy was to help him. Mama told me I could stay at home in Sister's and Mary Young's care or stay with Lizzie as I chose.

I dragged out my old knapsack, stuffed some clothes in it and my canteen. I dug out the money I had been saving to equip the boat—I planned to get a ship's spyglass and a cutlass. I smuggled the knapsack out and hid it in some bushes in the backyard. After supper I made a stack of sandwiches to add to the lumpy knapsack. I rose early to eat breakfast with Mama and Daddy and apparently listen to Mama's final admonishments. I explained to Mary Young that I might spend the nights at Lizzie's house, but I would be at Bup's all day until late. Then I skipped across to Lizzie's house, ate some cookies, and gabbled my vague intentions, which mentioned the possibility of spending the night with Bup. Grabbing my knapsack, I trotted around to Bup's, stopping to leave the knapsack in a lumber pile at Mr. Warner's.

Mary Young left her kitchen when she saw Lizzie come outside. "That boy up to somethin', Miss Lizzie," she said. "He's talkin' too much and rushin' around."

Lizzie pondered a moment, "I think you're right. I'll see what I can find out. We'd both better check on him."

I dashed in Bup's yard in time to help him and Macon and John Litchfield (Macon's helper) load the icebox on the store truck. We all rode to Mr. Warner's where Cap'n Ike and his mate rigged a boom and swung the heavy box onto the deck. Cap'n Ike told Bup he was sailing for Ocracoke as soon as he tested something or other, I did not understand what. They would load some lumber, too. Bup started home after I told him I would see him later, probably tomorrow. Some other men began to load a small pile of boards on *Russell L.'s* deck.

I retrieved my knapsack and casually wandered on board and over to the icebox. I removed the cork from the drainpipe and stuck it in my pocket. I dropped the knapsack in the icebox, and when nobody was looking jumped in myself. I had brought a piece of wood to stick under the lid, leaving a crack to peer through. I chose the ice compartment because it did not have a hasp on the lid nor any shelves inside. The stowaway was all set. I hoped I could "work my passage," as boys did in some of the sea stories.

After a while I heard the engine start and sensed that the ship was moving. I could not see much through my vision slit. I told myself that an experienced boat builder would be useful to Cap'n Ike on the trip and to Cap'n Dave on the trip back. I had enough money to pay the two dollars for my passage if I had to, but I did not want to. It would be easy to find a place to sleep and lots of people I knew would likely invite me to meals. I smiled at the new zinc liner.

Through the crack under the lid, I saw the heavy girders on the draw move by as the boat passed through the railroad bridge. The boat began to pitch a little, but I was too excited to feel seasick, or to nap. I thought I would have to stay in the box for at least an hour, or maybe two.

Russell L. chugged down the river. I wished I could see more. The wind was too light for sailing, but I could sense from the boat's motion that the river was wider and the waves bigger. The ship slowed and heeled a little to one side. She rolled more briefly, then stabilized and resumed speed. I could not tell what was happening or where we were. Minutes dragged by. I pushed the lid a little more open and peered all around. What was that I saw? It was the railroad bridge again, the tall draw overhanging the boat. We had turned around, I realized, and were going back to the dock.

I slumped down to worry. The boat slowed, swerved, the engine reversed, and then cut off. Another peep out showed me the mate with a rope in his hand preparing to heave it. As soon as we docked I scrambled out as fast as I could and crouched in the space between the icebox and the cabin. I thought nobody had seen me. On the dockside I saw a new pile of lumber.

Mr. Warner came up from the cabin, shook hands with Cap'n Ike and said, "The stuffin' box is all right. Didn't leak even a cup-full, and that right at first. I put the floorboards back."

I realized that it had been a test run. I stayed in place, still determined to sail to Ocracoke. Captain Ike walked forward, stood by the icebox, and gazed up at the masthead. "Mac," he said, without looking at me, "Your grandfather's on the dock. You'd better go ashore now." Cap'n Ike had never called me by name before. I wondered when he had spotted me. When I stood up and grabbed my knapsack, the captain grinned at me and waved goodbye.

I jumped ashore and trudged over to stand beside Bup, not knowing what to expect. How did Bup find out? He draped his arm over my shoulder and told me to come to the house. Bup did not mention stowaways, but talked about boats and wood and the weather. We sat in the swing by the new skiff. Bup changed the subject, and began to look serious as he told me something else. "Miss Lizzie telephoned me this morning. Since you're stay-ing with me, she invited us both to take dinner with her."

"Oh so that's it," I thought.

"Come on in the house and get cleaned up. Have you got a clean shirt in your satchel? I've got to get dressed, too." Bup put on a suit and tie and his spare glasses with the black silk cord on them. He looked different. We walked together to Aunt Lizzie's without talking much.

I did not enjoy that dinner even though Lizzie had prepared things I liked. We had roast lamb, Lizzie's special mashed potatoes, and spinach. My appetite was hearty, but I took no joy in the meal. Lizzie and Bup seemed to enjoy themselves a lot. They were very formal in addressing each other, saying "Miss Lizzie" and "Mr. McIlhenny." Bup told Lizzie a rambling story of a cousin who had run away by hitching a ride on the steam cars. Bup sometimes called a train "steam cars," which I thought was as odd as Lizzie's calling a truck a dray. The cousin's mother, Bup said, had nervous prostration and the doctor had to give her laudanum. He never did say if the cousin came home.

Lizzie countered with the tale of a relative who had an operation in a hospital in California. He did not write for weeks and his family worried all that time, not even knowing if he was alive. Lizzie observed that it was fortunate that I was not that thoughtless. Lizzie and Bup told other accounts of callous children and distraught families. They seemed to enjoy the misery they discussed. I was certainly miserable.

Aunt Lizzie served "Devil Cake," my favorite, for dessert. I did not want it, but I ate it. All I wanted was to get away from that table. At last Bup took his leave, telling Miss Lizzie how much he had enjoyed the meal and the visit. She told Mr. McIlhenny to please come back, and if any problems ever arose, she was sure the two of them could find solutions.

And that was all I ever heard about my extra trip to Ocracoke, except Mary Young's silent signs of disapproval. She sadly shook her head when I passed through her kitchen, or else glared at me, though in a few hours she sweetened up. There was one unforeseen benefit from the episode: Captain Ike waved and grinned at me whenever we met thereafter.

DULTRY

I DID NOT ENJOY THAT MONTH at Ocracoke as much as previous summers. Thoughts of the boat kept intruding. She was almost ready for launching and I wanted to be two places at once—at Ocracoke and in Bup's backyard working. I found plenty of things to do on the island and the house-party girls were entertaining as usual, but I was distracted.

Another distraction was puberty, though I did not know the word. Besides my special new words, I had learned a lot of terminology on the school grounds, with the gang in the neighborhood, and even in Sunday School. While our teacher was reading the Ten Commandments, we stopped her by asking what a "Dultry" was. One boy said if he did not even know what a Dultry was, how could he not commit one? She stammered and sweated and read on, but we had ascertained the meaning of our new word. I had seen pigs coupling at the farm and dogs "hung up" backwards, so I was not entirely ignorant, but I did not think people did it that way. I was curious.

When one girl visitor told me men and women made babies by rubbing their navels together, I did not believe it any more than the story of the stork. I knew men and ladies had different parts that somehow fitted together (probably like pintles and gudgeons), but I did not know much more. Avid to learn, I suggested to the girl that we take off our clothes and she could show me. I was half-afraid she would get mad and half-scared she might agree to do it. She scorned my suggestion, and told me she sure did not want a baby. That was the end of it just then, for any physical urge was latent at that age, but mentally I was eager to learn more. It was talk about signal flags that helped me learn.

I had always liked flags. With Lizzie's help I had flown the American flag in front of the house on George Washington's birthday and on Armistice Day. We displayed the Confederate flag on Memorial Day. I spent the fourth of July at Ocracoke, but never remembered to take a flag to fly there. The lighthouse and the Coast Guard station flew American flags, as did the Coast Guard's boats. The picket boat that searched for smuggled rum that time flew the National flag at the mast head and the special Coast Guard flag with up and down stripes at the stern. The big Coast Guard cutters displayed those same flags and had a special mast for different looking signal flags. Lee explained to me that you could say whole sentences with just a few signal flags, but you had to have a signal book to read them.

When the house-party girls started laughing to themselves about signal flags on a certain lady's clothesline, I perked up and began to pay attention. Sometimes the girls liked to talk craziness and I thought this was one of the times—signal flags on a clothesline! But I decided to check it out anyway.

They had mentioned Mrs. Smith, and I knew where she lived, on the little road that ran back of the Sound-front cottages. Her house was right where the road forked, with one branch leading 'round the Creek, and one going back to Mr. Wesson's store on the main road. There was no way a ship could see any signal flag on Mrs. Smith's clothesline.

I began to use the back road whenever I hiked 'round the Creek or to Wesson's store so I could check the clothesline. The first two times I passed nothing hung on the line; the next time it was full of Mr. and Mrs. Smith's clean clothes, but no flags.

The following Monday, with Mr. Smith back out on the deep-sea trawler, the line held Mrs. Smith's washing only: some dresses, a nightgown, and a lot of underwear. Had anybody been with me, I would have been embarrassed to stare at the underwear. Returning from my errand, I saw Mrs. Smith feeling her clothes to see if they were dry. We exchanged hellos. I glanced back and saw Mrs. Smith do a funny thing. She took the clothes pins off her nightgown and re-hung it upside down. That set me wondering, so I turned off the road and headed through the bushes to a big live oak growing nearer the Sound shore.

From a crotch high in the tree, I could see Mrs. Smith's yard, Wesson's store up one trail, and almost to the Creek the other way. Twisting around backwards, I looked at Mr. Bragg's house and Bup's cottage. The tree made a good observation post, so I wiggled down to fit the limbs and gazed around. No signal flags were flapping anywhere that I could see.

In a little while Mr. Wesson, toting a paper bag, crossed the porch of his store, skipped down the steps, and entered the trail. He halted, looked all around, then hurried along to the Smith's porch. I saw a loaf of bread in the bag as Mr. Wesson slipped in the door. I thought that might be what the laundry flag signalled, but it sure was a funny way to order a loaf of bread. I wondered how Mrs. Smith would order a jar of pickles, or whether, if she wanted a watermelon she would fly a great big flag: she could not display a bed sheet upside down. I stayed in the perch nearly an hour. As I began to climb down, Mr. Wesson popped out the door and headed back to his store.

I thought about telling Sister and the girls how Mrs. Smith used her clothesline to order groceries, but decided to wait until I learned more. A tiny doubt lurked in my mind.

The following day I inspected the clothesline and saw the same nightgown, or one like it, hanging by itself and upside down. I ducked in the bushes, but had not even reached the tree when Mr. Wesson trotted up the path and disappeared in Mrs. Smith's door. He was not carrying anything that time. Maybe he was going to get a grocery list of things she could not order by flag.

Mrs. Smith sure washed a lot of clothes, not so many at a time, but something almost every day. Whenever she hung the upside down thing, Mr. Wesson soon came to get the grocery order or to deliver it. The next week Mr. Smith was in port, for all his clothes hung on the line along with his wife's right-side-up laundry. Mr. Wesson did not deliver that week. I guessed Mr. Smith took care of the groceries himself.

One afternoon I cut over to the observation tree from the Sound side to see if I could spot the mail boat coming in. I did not notice the upside down gown at first. A familiar noise drew my attention that way, for Sister, Evelyn, Charlotte, and Wookie were heading 'round the Creek, talking, laughing, and giggling. After I saw the girls, I glanced at the store just in time to see Mr. Wesson jump off his porch to enter the trail. As soon as Mr. Wesson caught sight of the girls he wheeled around and scuttled back in his store. When the girls chattered off in the distance, Mr. Wesson trotted out again as Mrs. Smith opened the door.

At the supper table one of the girls said something about the clothesline signal and the rest of them laughed. I decided I would show off some by telling them what I knew about the signal flag and see what I could learn from their remarks. I would tell them about my first idea of the signal and not the real reasoning I had developed. I bragged that I knew what the signals meant: Mrs. Smith was ordering groceries by flag signal and Mr. Wesson was delivering them. My pearl of wisdom met with jeers from the girls until Mama silenced them.

I had learned long ago that Mama's eyebrows were signal flags for her mood. When she was happy her eyebrows formed nice bows. If she was worried or puzzled, her eyebrows turned up at the inside ends and crinkled. When she got mad the ends pointed down and signalled danger. They pointed down and she spoke in her severe voice.

"I've told you all to stop that silly gossiping. I mean it. Drop the subject from now on. And you, young man, mind your own business and don't concern yourself with other people's clothes-lines." She shook her finger under my nose. I had become cal-loused to many corrections, but I recognized "young man" as a danger signal like Mama's eyebrows. I shut up about the signals, but I did not forget them.

I was not as ignorant as I pretended to be with my smart talk. I did know what they were doing in there, and thought it must be fun because Mr. Wesson came so often. What I did not know was just how they performed—the exact technique. Lee was right, you could say a lot with just a few flags. I wished I had a complete signal book to explain it all.

I did not expect to learn any more about the technique of what Smith and Wesson did until I could talk to some of the older boys at home, and I did not. I certainly did not expect to learn that any of the people at the house party were doing what Smith and Wesson did.

I stood on the shore early one morning watching a skipjack skipping through the waves from across the Sound. She rounded the shoal and sailed along the shore to turn in the Creek. I was late for breakfast. Before I sat down at my place, I knew some-thing was wrong. Mama snapped at me, "Sit down and eat your breakfast," as she passed me the platter of bacon and fried eggs. I decided not to complain about cold eggs because Mama's eye-brows once more signalled trouble. They pointed at the floor. Her eyes, usually large, brown, and merry, were black and squinched half-shut. Her compressed lips spoke slowly and precisely. She was in a cold fury, something I had rarely seen. I was satisfied it was not directed at me, so I kept my mouth shut and listened hard, while I picked at cold eggs and bacon. Sister and the other girls sat silently and looked scared.

Only one of the girls seemed different. Gladys had her chair pushed back and held her cup and saucer in a rattling clutch. She was red-faced and clamp-jawed, and acted indignant.

Mama spoke again, to Gladys, "I think you could have informed me."

"It was too late to send anybody with a message by then," Gladys answered, "so I just stayed with them until I felt better this morning."

"And you!" Mama glared at Sister and each of the other girls in turn. "You told me nothing. When you all came in and went upstairs I assumed all was well. You told me nothing. I have not had to count heads or call the roll before this."

"Yes'm," was all they could stammer.

Shifting her fire back to Gladys, Mama continued, "If I hadn't seen you with your shoes in your hand, I don't suppose I'd have known when you came in. Thomina's chaperoning that house party. Surely she would have let me know if one of my girls was there sick."

Gladys interrupted. "Miss Nita, she didn't even know I was there. I felt bad and went on in to bed, just like I told you."

"Your mothers put you in my charge when you came here, and I intend to be in charge. Now all of you clear out. I'll get to the bottom of this before I'm through."

The girls scattered. I gulped the rest of my cold eggs while Mama drank coffee, smoked cigarettes, and drummed her fingers on the table. Her face remained hard as she stared off into space. I crept out to sit under Mr. Bragg's pier to consider this new situation.

I was suspicious. Gladys's boyfriend Humphrey had come to the island. He stayed at the Pamlico Inn, but he had hung around the cottage all the previous day with Gladys and went to the square dance with her that night. Just spending the night at

Miss Thomina's cottage was not something to get that mad about. There must have been more. Were Gladys and Humphrey delivering groceries like Smith and Wesson? I could not ask and still had no signal book.

I had invented a special name for Gladys one time I saw all the girls swimming nekkid. I had walked out of the bushes way past Springer's Point and there they were. They all squalled "Go away!" so I wheeled around and ran. Gladys was the closest one, standing in knee-deep water looking at me. The hair on her head was dark red, but the hair down there on her gudgeon was just brown. She reminded me of a cat I once had with patches of different colored fur all over it. I had named the cat Hash. I thought of Gladys as Hashcat ever after. I never called her that, though.

Humphrey did not come back to the cottage. I saw him and Hashcat talking on the path to the turtle bridge later that day. One of the girls said he took the next boat home. Humphrey was tall and slim, with a head not much wider than his neck. I decided to name him Eel.

Mama seemed to get over her anger, though I was still curious, and noticed she did not talk much to Gladys any more. I did not hear any more about Hashcat and Eel until way in the next summer, and then not very much.

Mr. Bragg came over to the cottage later that month, which was unusual, for Mr. Bragg did not take time to visit. I remembered seeing him at the cottage just once before, the time Mama thought I was lost at sea. Mr. Bragg introduced the man with him as Bob Something, his wife's niece's brother-in-law, and a house builder. Bob said "pleased to meetcha" and Mr. Bragg asked permission to look around the cottage. He said he had talked to Bup about it.

Mama invited him to look around as he pleased, and did not seem surprised. She called to Sister and said Gary Bragg and Bob

Something wanted to look upstairs. Mr. Bragg told her they would check the outside of the house first, so he walked around the side. I followed him, curious as ever.

Bob Something came, too, carrying a long, sharp pointed iron rod with a short wood handle on the other end. Bob ducked under the house dragging his single-barrel gig behind him. I followed. I had crawled under the house before this and had noted the great big sills under the main walls. Bup had once told me that some of the big oak timbers had come from a shipwreck on the beach. I liked to think it was Blackbeard's ship. Bob puffed his way under the cottage and began to jab his gig in the timbers. The gig made a solid "tunk" in the wood. When he reached the middle and jabbed the big sill, the sound was almost a clang. "Jesus", Bob grunted, and rubbed his elbow. Bob was thorough. He tunked and clanged along, all the way to the other side. "Its all solid," he reported to Mr. Bragg.

They looked over the backyard, then climbed the porch steps. Mr. Bragg patted the lid of the icebox as he told Bob about it. Next he seized the pump handle to pump up a good flow of the darkish water. Bob cupped his hands and drank some, promptly spitting it out; Mr. Bragg knew better.

Mama met them in the kitchen and showed them the rest of the downstairs rooms. The girls all had come down and were perched around the porch, so Mama asked Sister to show Mr. Bragg and Bob the upstairs rooms. I did not follow them there, for I had not been welcome upstairs since the time I left the hard crabs under the beds. Mr. Bragg thanked Mama and Sister for showing him the house, then he and Bob went home.

Mama turned to Sister and said, "Gary Bragg's been trying to buy the cottage from Papa. I expect he'll make another offer now."

That was a new thought for me to chew on. I did not like the idea of selling the cottage to anybody. I did realize it was Bup's business and not mine. There were, after all, other cottages.

It was almost time to go 'round the Creek to meet the mailboat. I thought I might get another letter from Lee in New Orleans. I looked for Sister to see if the girls were going.

It had been a pretty good summer even though neither Lee nor Billy was there. My Ocracoke buddy Johnny stayed just a week with his uncle, but I was not bored, with all the interesting things that occurred.

I completed one special project. I had brought the two little squares of scrap icebox liner that Macon had cut out for me. Rummaging out some paint from the old shipyard supplies, I made name boards for the new boat. Painting the zinc pieces white and on them, in dark red, the name *Bup*, I tried to copy all the fancy printing I had ever seen—not worrying that it was so fancy it was hardly legible. I anticipated fastening the name plates on the bow and Bup's pride in seeing them.

THE ARTS
& ENTERTAINMENT

WE DID NOT JUST GO from cottage to Sound, to ocean, to dance pavillion, and thence back home. There were lots of other things to do, even better then searching for Down Below. The girls invented a lot of pastimes, and visitors brought more.

There was singing. Sometimes in the pavillion Zoph or Mr. Jacobson would play popular songs in impromptu concerts and everybody (except me) would join in. Most often one of the girls would start it anywhere, on the beach truck, sitting on the pier, or on the cottage porch. One summmer a visiting boy brought a ukulele and that helped a lot, but that was not really necessary. A lot of the songs were crazy imitations of radio singers ("a burlesque of a serious song" Uncle Thomas Hill called it).

The song Sister liked best was a sad one about a young lady getting drowned. She sang it in a country accent—and since we were country folk ourselves, it was from deep in the country. The young lady's name was Nellie and "twas on the twentieth of November her cruel lover pushed her into the waters deep and cold." We never did get her out in that song, but she kept getting pushed in.

There were other sad ones, but there were some lively songs, too. One of the Pantegonians, I can't remember which one, brought a banjo which really pepped up the singing. That banjo could not play sad tunes like poor Nellie. There was a song about someone named Nellie Gray that I mixed up with twentieth of November Nellie.

Sister's high school class attended a ballet in Raleigh, so burlesque ballet dancing was added to the Ocracoke fine arts program. One of the island boys named it "Op'ry dancing."

Painting was on the island arts program at times. Sister and Cousin Helene decorated the envelopes of their correspondence with each other all year round with Ocracoke scenes, barely leaving room for the address. Theirs was interesting-looking mail.

One summer a real, professional artist came to see us, Mr. Giles. Young artists had a hard time making a living in those depression years. Jessie Giles of Washington, N.C. was out of work and energetic in looking around. He worked for a time out west at Mount Rushmore helping to chisel presidents' heads out of a mountain side. I think that came later, after his Ocracoke visits. At the island, he would paint little seaside scenes on the inside of large clam shells. His shell art was not a real picture, but just a hint of what he saw, but they sold. One of the girls said it was his impression of things. In any case, he caused the shipyard to shift to art for a while.

Mr. Giles was not really responsible for the atrocities we committed, but he inspired us. We had a stock of four-hour enamel paint, some brushes, and unbounded confidence in our ability. We were not impressionists—we tried to put in every detail. I found a sample of my clamshell art years later. It depicted the Sound shore from Mr. Bragg's pier to Springer's Point, with Cap'n Bill's pier, the dance pavillion, the oil tanks, the front of the Inn, and Springer's house—it was a full clamshell. I had to admit that Mr. Giles's work looked better.

Once in a while the girls and visiting boys would hold a weenie roast on the beach. Adults did not attend these cook-outs, but the girls let me and my buddy come. We ate hot dogs, marshmallows, or anything that could be cooked on a stick. One of the Belhaven boys offered to cook fish for us the way the Indians cooked, on a grid made of green twigs. His grid caught fire and collapsed. He did manage to cook a portion of fish speared on a stick like a hot dog, but his fish usually managed to go from raw to burned-up in a flash. Some of the boys learned to barbeque fish on a green-wood grid set back from hot coals, but most of them used a frying pan. We never held a clam bake, possibly because nobody was very good at raking clams. Lee and I had the clam rakes Mr. Credle had given us, but we could never find many clams (except in Mr. Bragg's clam-bed).

There was never a lack of things to do on the island, especially at a house party like ours. We seemed to have fun "makin' fun" of anything.

HOMEWARD BOUND

THE SCENIC VOYAGE HOME in the daytime had always been a fitting conclusion to the month on the island. This year, I had decided, I would watch carefully everything that happened on the boat. As a future captain and ship owner I had to prepare for my new career. My grim determination helped me when I practiced scowling at the horizon. I did feel a little bit sad, as usual, when the island dwindled astern.

There were only two passengers aboard the *Preston*, besides the house party. Mama set up her headquarters on the front hatch as usual. The two Ocracokers who jumped aboard set their suitcases by the rear hatch and continued aft to the crew's cabin. They sat on its edge and spoke to Captain Dave and the mate. The girls arranged themselves on the hatch around Mama.

Just as the captain and the mate were preparing to cast off the mooring lines, someone shouted from the land end of Cap'n Bill's dock, "Wait, wait!" A fat man toting a big suitcase ran out on the dock. He was dressed all in white—in fact he was all white except for his pink face and his bright blue eyes. His smooth baby-face was a pleasing contrast to his mop of curly, white hair. He stood at the edge of the dock a minute, puffing and blowing, then carefully lowered himself to the deck. I thought he looked like one of Santa Claus's kids. The late arrival seemed shaky, so Cap'n Dave helped him with his bag and showed him the passenger cabin. The man said he would put his bag there, but would prefer to sit somewhere on deck. He saw that the front hatch was occupied, so he sat on the edge of the cabin.

The new passenger appraised Mama and the girls and smiled at them. He recognized Mama as boss of the group, stood up, made a little bow to her, and introduced himself as Lennie Post, the best shoe salesman on the east coast. He exuded politeness and jollity. He also exuded a faint odor of gin, but he was not close enough for anybody to detect it. Mama's invisible anti-alcohol antennae were erect and quivering, but they were not signalling anything. The girls giggled at Lennie's appearance. He did not seem pushy, just friendly, so Mama relaxed for the time being, but she remained watchful.

The *Preston* left the dock and began what looked like a calm crossing. The aspiring sea captain classified it as not a flat ca'm, but not sailing weather either. I watched Ocracoke recede until the lighthouse, a fat white stick glistening in the sun, was all I could identify. I made plans to ask Cap'n Dave to point out North Creek when we entered the mouth of the river. The Washington boat headed west across a smooth Sound.

The girls still posed on the hatch cover, talking and laughing about incidents of the past month. Mama was reading. I had a book, too, but I was more interested in the boat and the Sound than reading. Lennie Post carried his big suitcase down in the cabin, stayed a few minutes, then reappeared. A little while later he entered the cabin again. I wondered if he was using the marine toilet that was way up front in the cabin. I wanted to use it, which I did not mind doing when the cabin was empty. As the toilet was screened only by a canvas curtain, I felt uncomfortable with other passengers in the cabin. When I went below I saw Mr. Post's unstrapped suitcase lying on a bunk.

Lennie Post spent his time talking to the girls. He had a stock of funny stories, mostly crazy things that had happened to him during his travels selling shoes. Mama listened to him intently at first, to make sure he was not telling improper jokes. When Lennie had passed her smut test she resumed reading. The girls listened to his stories, though not all of them sat still. They were more like a flock of birds perched in a tree. Some took flight, changed formation, re-lit on different branches, then came back to the hatch. As the long Sound crossing continued, some of them were there to be entertained by Mr. Post. I listened for a while, then went forward to sit on the bowsprit and gaze ahead at the empty Sound. When I strolled aft I saw Lennie go in the cabin again, reappear, and commence telling a story about a man he knew named Soloman Sillietoe.

Hoping to be invited to stay, I wandered back to the rear cabin. Cap'n Dave was at the wheel; the mate and the two Ocracokers were sitting nearby. Nobody asked me to come on back, so I leaned against the mast and looked up at the sky and clouds. After a while Cap'n Dave called the mate to the steering wheel and started forward. He said hello to me. That was the right moment, so I asked Cap'n Dave if he would point out North Creek to me when we passed it, and explained why I wanted to look at it.

"I will," answered the captain. "Do ye' know Indian Island? Can ye' recognize it yourself?"

"Yes sir," I spouted. I remembered the island and a tale of an Indian massacre. It was way past the lighthouse beacon in the mouth of the river.

"When we get abreast of Indian Island come back here and I'll let you look through my glasses at North Creek," Cap'n Dave offered.

That delighted me. I poured a torrent of thanks on the captain before rushing back to the headquarters hatch to tell Mama and the girls what the captain had said.

206

Mama was pouring out the last of the lemonade from the big thermos jug. I took a cupful. She offered some to Mr. Post, who was climbing out of the cabin. He declined politely, telling her lemonade might make his hair turn white. The other thermos jug still had some iced tea. These two big insulated containers had been designed especially for the long boat trip to the island; Macon had built them in the tin shop at the store under Daddy's direction. Tin inside and copper outside with cork packed in between the two shells, they had leather-covered cork lids and a leather carrying strap. Each one held nearly two gallons, and they were square so they were easy to pack and store away. Mama capped the empty one and used it to prop up her book.

Mama and I read on, as there was nothing to see but water and sky. The girls lounged around, talking among themselves. Mr. Post snoozed on the cabin top. I read two or three chapters in my old Don Sturdy book before I noted a light breeze had begun to blow. It came from astern, fair for sailing. I remembered some of the grown-ups saying that Captain Dave and Captain Ike did not like to run their engines much, because gas was expensive. They preferred using sail and I agreed, not for economy, but because sailing was so much more fun than engine cruising.

Cap'n Dave, at the wheel, sent the mate forward to unbind the bundles of sails and get ready to hoist them. The two Ocracokers came along to help. They asked Lennie Post to move from the cabin top so they could work on the sail on the fore-mast. He descended into the cabin for a longer visit than usual. When he appeared once more, red-faced and grinning, he tried to get the girls attention. He went way past clowning into acting like a fool: wrong behavior on a boat. He tried to do a dance step along the rail—and danced himself right over the side.

We all saw him plunge. Cap'n Dave and Mama acted instant-ly, where the rest of us just gaped as Mr. Post floated belly up, looking like a white baby whale with big eyes and open mouth.

Cap'n Dave spun the steering wheel hard over, and the

Preston began a tight turn. He yelled at the mate to throw a life ring. The big life buoy the mate threw splashed down twenty feet short. Mama grabbed the empty cooler jug, and in a smooth continuous swivel, hurled it at Lennie Post. She almost hit him. Captain Dave kept *Preston* on her course, ready to begin another hard turn. Lennie Post, now clutching the thermos jug, with its strap around his neck, floated upright. The whale looked wild. The captain directed the three men to stand by on one side while he again turned *Preston* to close Mr. Post. He slowed the engine after he completed the turn, then took the propeller out of gear, all the while steering carefully. He judged the manoeuver exactly, for *Preston* lost headway just abreast of the floater and only a few feet to windward. The big bugeye, with engine idling, drifted gently down to him. The mate, held by one of the Ocracokers, hung over the side, grabbed Mr. Post's arm and tugged. The second man grasped Lennie's other arm and they heaved him up on deck. The white whale was rescued.

Captain Dave hurried forward to check his passenger's condition. Mr. Post tried to smile at the anxious captain, and said, "Shorry for the delay, Cap'm, but thish lady dropped her cobber boxsh overboard. I had to get it for her." If Captain Dave was taken aback by that explanation, he did not show it. He just looked grim. The two islanders cackled.

Mr. Post turned to Mama, unslung the cobber boxsh, and made a full bow. "Here dear lady, is your boxsh, rescued for you by L. Post, Eshquire."

Mama, struggling to appear solemn, answered, "Mr. Post, I really think you believe what you're saying. You need rest. Please sleep it off somewhere safe."

Captain Dave was not so polite to Mr. Post. He told him to go in the cabin and put on some dry clothes. Then he ordered himto stay in that cabin until he was told he could come out. Captain Dave sent one of the men with him to see that he carried out his orders. The Ocracoker came back on deck brandishing Lennie

Post's empty gin bottle. Mama's detection system had failed for the first time.

Captain Dave recovered the life ring, had the men hoist the sails, and shut down the engine. *Preston* slipped easily through the water, heeling a little to the light breeze. The wind, as if it had been waiting for the rescue to be completed, began to freshen.

Soon *Preston* was heeling way over, throwing spray from the bow, and threshing along in what I believed was the most exhilarating motion in the world. Mr. Post poked his head out of the cabin and waved to the captain. His face was pale, not pink. Captain Dave sent the mate forward to tell Lennie he could come on deck and sit on the rear hatch. The mate escorted him there and ordered him not to move anywhere else. When Lennie lay down, Mama sent me back with a rolled-up blanket he could use as a pillow. Mr. Post slept and gradually got his color back.

For me, the best part of the trip had begun, although the previous novel events had been exciting. I had met interesting characters on every trip to Ocracoke, for the island brought forth a sort of festive spirit in everyone. They were all different, most were nice, a few were bad, and only a few were drunk.

There was not much to see on the second half of the Sound crossing. We passed two shrimp trawlers at a distance, and way over toward the Hyde County shore I spied a skipjack heading across the Sound. The next sight to see, I knew, would be the Pamlico Light. It could not be called a landmark, and I did not think "watermark" was the right word either.

It was a powerful light marking Pamlico Point and the mouth of the river. The light was atop a neat little house that perched on tall pilings, way out in the water, barely in sight of land. It had a big railed-in area around it like a wood-floored yard and a small boat tied up underneath. It showed the river's mouth to mariners and illustrated a word for me: forever after, hearing or seeing the word lonesome, I thought of Pamlico Light.

I had a second thought, too, about something Cap'n Ike had said several years before. As the *Russell L.* passed the light that trip, Cap'n Ike pointed to the light-keeper leaning on the rail, "He raises everything he eats," he told one passenger. I thought that meant he had boxes of dirt with vegetables growing in them and maybe a pig pen and chicken coops. I tried to spot them the next time I passed the light. I thought about asking Cap'n Ike, but never had the opportunity. That summer, on the last trip home, I saw a big gas boat tied up to the piling with the men hoisting some boxes and bags up to the light house deck, and I understood Cap'n Ike's joke at last. I was glad I had not asked any dumb questions.

This light house was called the new Pamlico Light, as it had only been in use for some fifty years. After the *Preston* passed it, I knew I would see the old Pamlico Lighthouse on the first low sandy point. I stood by the rail, one hand on a foremast stay, trying to look salty, and gazing to windward. We passed the old light, a tumbled pile of bricks and some big chunks of stone, awash at the water's edge. Lizzie had told me the tower had been destroyed in the Civil War and somebody had carried the light and lens upriver to hide them from the Yankees. Anytime I explored an abandoned house, or a cellar, or an old store room, I hoped I would find the light and lens, but I never did.

A lump ahead in the river grew into Indian Island. In an hour we passed it and I went aft to the captain's cabin, where I stood by the water barrel, eager though still trying to look salty.

Captain Dave saw me, gave the mate the wheel, and beckoned me to come aft. The captain went down in the cabin and returned with a pair of binoculars in a leather case. He positioned me against the side of the cabin where I could look under the mainsail and across the river. He removed the glasses from their case and slipped their leather strap over my head. He adjusted the binoculars' width to my eyes and explained how to focus them. He pointed to the shore. "That's North Creek," Captain

Dave explained. "You'll see a post beacon in the mouth of the creek where the trees look lower. There's a house behind the point between the forks of the creek. Pamlico Beach is where you see those high bluffs off to your right. Cozzens Point is to the left—the tall pines. That's what ye want to look at. Don't drop the glasses."

I was full of the moment. I was actually on the quarterdeck of the Ocracoke boat, using the ship's glasses, and inspecting Daddy's new North Creek land. I picked out the marker in the mouth of the creek, shifted left, and saw tall pines and a pier. Traversing to the right, I inspected Pamlico Beach, then moved back to Cozzens Point. I considered it the best-looking piece of river shore.

It was not the ocean, but you could look out across the Sound to Ocracoke. The river was wide, and to Up Trent and Down Below, I added Indian Island as another place to explore. One of the Ocracokers told me he had been overnight in North Creek on a shrimper. "Good fishin' thar," he said. I returned the glasses to Cap'n Dave and thanked him as effusively as my shyness allowed.

I bounced back to the forward hatch to tell everybody what I had seen. I passed Mr. Post, still sleeping on the aft hatch, and looking like a big, parboiled red baby.

In too short a time, Captain Dave had the sails furled and started the engine. The *Preston* passed through the railroad trestle and the Ocracoke voyage was over for the summer. Over!

Daddy met us at the dock with the store truck and everybody scrambled for luggage. The house party hauled up most of it from the cabin while the mate handed me what was in the hold. One of Charlotte's brothers came in their big Buick to carry the girls home. The girls carried their small bags, but all the heavier bags and boxes were loaded on the truck.; they would get their other things later. Mama got in the cab with Daddy, and I sat on the back, legs dangling off the rear.

Before we could drive away, Mr. Post rushed up to introduce himself to Daddy. Then he spoke to Mama. Mr. Post was a gentleman—a sober gentleman. "I think you saved my life," he said, "and I'm grateful. I'd like to go back to that island again some day. I hope to meet you all again." Indeed, Mr. Post was an irrepressible gentleman, for he said, "If we meet again on the Ocracoke boat, I guarantee you'll think I'm a Sunday-school superintendent on the way home from a Prohibition Convention."

He asked the way to the bus station, so Daddy offered him a ride. He sat on the back with me and told me a tale about a man named J. Wellington Frogbottom, Jr., whose right foot was twice as big as his left foot. In the cab, Mama told Daddy all about Mr. Post's accident. "Another highland terrapin and a drunk one," Daddy laughed.

Back home at last, I rushed through my part of the truck unloading. I trotted to the kitchen to check in with Mary Young, then ran over to Lizzie's house. She was preparing supper but was willing to sit down and hear about the island. I told her quickly about the man who almost got drowned, promised to give a full report on the island later, and did not tarry. I galloped around to Bup's house to check on the boat. It, or she, was in good condition, still on the saw horses, and covered with canvas. I promised to tell Bup all the news the next morning. I went home to eat my supper and went to bed early.

The series of events that ended the Ocracoke summers occurred during the following weeks. The first shock was the news that Bup had sold the big cottage to Gary Bragg. I had been given some warning of it the day Mr. Bragg and Bob Something had looked at the house, but I had put that visit in the memories of things I wanted to forget. There would be still Bup's other cottage and Aunt Ella's cottage. I thought Mr. Bragg would still let us swim from his pier. I enjoyed imagining that whoever lived at

Mr. Swillingham Three's address might come to the new people in the cottage, demanding a tour of the island, and how puzzled everybody would be.

The next Sunday afternoon Daddy drove us to look at the North Creek land. He showed Mama where he would build a camp. Mama said if it was a comfortable camp, she would like to stay there some in the summer. Daddy said he would add rooms as he could afford them. The new land was to be a profit-making venture, as Daddy and Mr. Cozzens planned to sell lots. Daddy told me I would have a job that winter when Mr. Wallace, Lee's daddy, surveyed the lots. I wanted to know all about surveying, so Daddy explained it. "You're not old enough to operate a transit, but you can operate a bush ax and pull a chain," he added.

A few days later, after supper, Mama told the family she thought it would be best if they did not plan to go to Ocracoke the next summer. "Papa's other cottage is rented all summer and Ella's is unsettled. Besides," she told Daddy, "some of the girls are getting hard to handle." I knew she was talking about Gladys, the hashcat. We left the table and Mama, Daddy, and Sister sat on the side porch to talk some more. Sammy went off. I wanted solitude to consider this new development, which struck me like a doomsday announcement.

I trudged out in the backyard and climbed the same old Otaheite tree that grew by the barn. I jammed my backside in the big crotch that I called my spy post. It was a tight fit, for I had grown more than the tree during the Ocracoke years. I could not imagine a summer without Ocracoke. I would never make the Up Trent camping safari, nor see Springer's Point and the Doxsee house again. I could never visit Portsmouth. Never again to visit Cap'n Bill's or Pointer Beach or the ocean seemed near 'bout like death. I crouched in gloom for nearly five minutes.

My mood brightened considerably when I recollected Bup had told me to come around to finish some touch-up painting and to varnish the oars. Bup wanted me there when he installed the oarlocks. Launching day was near, so thoughts of the island faded. I still had not put on the name plates and I wanted to see how Bup liked them.

Mama, Daddy, Lizzie, Sister, Bup, and even Sammy came to the launching. We carried the *Bup* on the store truck to Mr. Emory's shop and launched her there. Sister started cheering, so everybody joined in, including Mr. Emory and his helpers. The *Bup* rowed like a dream, fast and easy to manage, the best handling skiff I had ever rowed.

I thought everybody would want a ride, but Daddy said the first voyage should be for me and Mr. Mac. Bup took his seat in the stern and commented, "I'm ready when you are, Captain." We shoved off, through the draw, heading for the creek behind Aunt Annie's house, where I would keep her. Bup was nearly as pleased with the boat as I was.

The gloom that had enveloped me up in the crotch of the Otaheite tree did not return. I had learned that although good times may seem everlasting, things can change and be replaced by new and better times.

New vistas opened for me. There was North Creek—Pinecrest as Daddy had named it—to explore, and Indian Island and all the river shore in between. I promised myself that I would get a bigger boat when I was older, so I could go to Ocracoke whenever I wanted to. I would sail to Portsmouth ("Porchmouth" as the Ocracokers pronounced it), and to Down Below. I could sail to Hatteras to drink some of that "forty-fathom" coffee, and sail outside if we sighted a Portagee schooner. There was still a lot to do.

A CAROLINA CHILDHOOD
BOOK 1

HIGH DAYS & HOLIDAYS
Scenes from a Tyrrell County Childhood

STEP BACK IN TIME to a small village in rural northeastern North Carolina in the '20s and '30s where the Liverman family store was the local gathering place where tales were told, jokes shared, and problems solved.

MEET *Democrat* the mule, *Hoover* the kitten, and *Woodrow Wilson* the irascible tom—beloved animals of men whose passions ran high and loyalties deep. Take a ride in a 1923 Model T Ford sedan, a Maxwell touring car, or a buggy drawn by *Annie* the claybank mare. Share a young boy's delight in the fun and flavors of a midwinter hog killing, the terror of a trip to the tonsil clinic, and the high jinks at a hoedown where "the fur flew" and the *Joe Reek Boys* first played!

JOE LIVERMAN, a doctor in neighboring Hyde County, has never forgotten his boyhood days nor the beloved characters of his native Tyrrell County. In this collection of stories he has vividly recreated a bygone era with his sharp eye, wry sense of humor, and the skill of a born storyteller.

available from Sweet Bay Tree Books, Columbia, NC 27925-0100
or by e-mail at sweetbaytreebooks@hotmail.com